Leaving Guanabara

Denise B. Dailey

Momentum Ink Press

New York

Published in the United States by Momentum Ink Press, New York.

PUBLISHER'S CATALOGING-IN-PUBLICATION DATA

Names: Dailey, Denise B., author.
Title: Leaving Guanabara / Denise B. Dailey.
Identifiers: 978-0-9994069-2-2 (hardcover) | 978-0-9994069-4-6 (paperback) | 978-0-9994069-3-9 (Kindle ebook)
Subjects: LCSH: Brazil--Biography. | French--Foreign countries. | Guanabara Bay (Brazil) | Coming of age. | Family secrets. | World War, 1939-1945--Biography. | BISAC: BIOGRAPHY & AUTOBIOGRAPHY / Personal Memoirs.
Classification: LCC F2538.5.D35 A3 2019 (print) | LCC F2538.5.D35 (ebook) | DDC 981.06/092--dc23.

Printed in the United States of America

For information about special discounts available for bulk purchases, sales promotions, fund-raising and educational needs, contact the author at daileytd@aol.com

http://denisebdailey.com
https://momentuminkpress.com

Also by Denise B. Dailey, available on Amazon: *Listening to Pakistan: A Woman's Voice in a Veiled Land* and *Riko: Seductions of an Artist*.

Book design by Katie Holeman | https://kshcreative.com

à nos aïeux
à ma soeur
à nos enfants

Elizabeth Bishop's *One Art*

The art of losing isn't hard to master;
so many things seem filled with the intent
to be lost that their loss is no disaster.

Lose something every day. Accept the fluster
of lost door keys, the hour badly spent.
The art of losing isn't hard to master.

Then practice losing farther, losing faster;
places, and names, and where it was you meant
to travel. None of these will bring disaster.

I lost my mother's watch. And look! My last, or
next-to-last, of three loved houses went.
The art of losing isn't hard to master.

I lost two cities, lovely ones. And, vaster,
some realms I owned, two rivers, a continent.
I miss them, but it wasn't a disaster.

Even losing you (the joking voice, a gesture
I love) I shan't have lied. It's evident
the art of losing's not too hard to master
though it may look like (*Write* it!) like disaster.

Table of Contents

Prologue

Our father used to sing a song that, in retrospect, became emblematic of the war years for me, *Tout va très bien, Madame la Marquise.* The song is about the Marquise who calls home to her château after a fortnight away to find out how things are going. In fact, everything is being destroyed but the response from her majordomo, her stable hand and her other helpers is that everything is fine ("Tout va très bien"). They are keeping secrets from her. I didn't think to ask why.

The war I refer to is the Second World War, the place Brazil, where the Otis Elevator Company had stationed our father, and where my sister, Arlette, and I were born. As the second daughter of a French father and a Chilean-French mother, I lapped up the stew of different indigenous and ex-patriot nationalities, their languages, music, cultures and sensibilities. Arlette, and I were treated to the banquet of Brazil and its gentle, generous people with whom we formed quick and deep ties. Even then, we knew we were living in a paradise.

In the meantime, in northern Africa, Russia, Asia, the Pacific and Europe, war raged. Unknown to Arlette or to me, it annihilated the worlds of our unmet paternal grandparents in Paris and Bordeaux when these cities fell under the German and Vichy regimes. In time, their losses became ours and we went on to learn new ones.

PART ONE

The War Years

1940 – 1945

CHAPTER ONE

Imaginings

The Brazilians say the only way to cure deep longings is to kill them, *matar saudades*. It doesn't work. I've tried.

* * *

"Look at this." Arlette passed me a photo. "I found it in the trunk Daddy brought from Rio. It surfaced when I was mucking about in his basement the other day, and the wonder is, that after nearly thirty-five years, everything in it wasn't moldy."

The photograph shows our mother sitting backwards on a horse, my father sitting forwards on the following horse, the better to hear each other's voices. Our parents are both young, smiling, and it looks as if our mother is the one speaking. There is a German shepherd on the trail near our father's horse, so we guessed two things: first, the picture was taken in Santiago where our mother's family kept horses and where she rode frequently; second, it was before our parents married and moved to Brazil because, by then, our father had given up his beloved dog, Mary, too jealous of our father's attentions to our mother (a confession our father made with still evident pain many years later). But almost everything else is conjecture; we know so little about our parents.

"That's Mummy's mother," Arlette said, pulling out a small photograph from the stack and handing it to me. Perhaps it was taken for an official purpose as the name, 'Emma Bottin,' was scrawled on the back. Without that identification, I should not have claimed the graying-haired woman, with her hair pulled back, who turns a pleasant full gaze in my direction. Similarly with our grandfather whose name, Louis Bottin, was scratched in fine lettering on the back of his photo. His eyes crinkled at the facing camera, but his bushy moustache hid any smile.

The photographs are headshots of two middle-aged people, nothing more. We had no context to place them in, no clean or messy kitchen in which to stand our grandmother, no harp or piano behind which to sit her, no knitting to hide her lap, no desk littered with a game of solitaire or with letters she was answering.

As to our grandfather, we could not see if he was in a garden or indoors, if a dog or a bee hive hummed at his side, whether his fingers were gnarled or straight, if his wedding band still fit, if a vest or homespun sweater (with a moth hole or two?) warmed him. We could not see if his fingernails were clean and filed, or cracked and earth-filled. We didn't know if the photos came from their years in France or from their years in Chile.

From the upper layers of the trunk, bit by bit, Arlette had unpacked and set aside Chilean silver in the form of goblets we used to drink from on special occasions; horse brasses and bridle decorations that hung on the wall of our entrance in Rio; the *chicote*—the leather horse whip Mummy carried with her when she rode; a pair of heavy, intricately carved wooden stirrups the Chilean gauchos used; a straight mahogany canoe paddle with the top carved in the shape of a head; two male figures—one a thin-featured hunchback, the other a taller almost totemic human with a flat face—carved by either the Mapuche or the Araucanian Indians. The carvings used to sit near our sofa in the living room. There were a few blue- and red-patterned ceramic platters, bowls and dishes from China that somehow had come to our mother, plus an album with letters and a sketchy journal from her years at Oberlin College. (How had she got there?)

Our father had filled the trunk in 1950 when he closed our home in Rio after our mother died. In the same way that he had sequestered his family and life growing up in France, he would not speak of our mother or of our life in Brazil ever again, so Arlette and I were particularly glad to have the artifacts he saved from her life in Chile, what she brought to their marriage, but family tales were missing.

By the time Arlette discovered the trunk, it was 1984. We were seated in the living room of her sheep farm in Georgeville, Quebec, where she, her husband, Tony, and their three children had settled. I, too, was married with three children, but living in New York City, so my meetings with Arlette were few, our speaking about our life in Brazil rare. "I don't like to talk about it," Arlette would say. I respected her boundaries, but my curiosity festered.

I chose to go on a journey of three continents to explore the context of those years. I reconstructed from letters and a college scrap album I had of our mother's, what she might have written to her family in Chile, not so far off from Brazil, but unreachable during those war years of travel restrictions. We knew there could have been scant correspondence with our father's family in France under the German Occupation.

The process of assembling the narrative became like my compulsive picking away at a scab. It was sometimes satisfying, sometimes painful, and I ignored the original wound that needed to protect itself with the cover I was willing to destroy. I slipped back to when my own memories were clear. I started with one event we shared with equal lucidity: World War II.

When victory in Europe was announced, Rio exploded in sambas, confetti, the perfume of ether sprays, and an orchestra of native and expatriate voices. In our house, my parents danced the *cueca* on the dark rosewood dining room table. The seductive dance of small steps my mother brought from Chile had a syncopation that night of joyous foot stompings and shouts of glee. Our dark-haired father was laughing so hard, it sounded like hiccups, and our blond mother looked especially petite next to his tall athletic form. My parents hugged each other. They hugged Arlette. They hugged me, and then they danced some more.

Their unbridled delight was fun to see, but disturbing. I had loved the war years.

CHAPTER TWO

Training for War
1940

Jornal do Brazil

Rio de Janeiro—Domingo, 23 de Junho de 1940

Firmado o armisticio entre a França e Alemanha

June 23, 1940—France signs armistice with Germany

Letter from our mother to her family in Santiago.

June, 1940—São Paulo

Querida familia,

In less than a month, the Jornal do Brasil *has declared that the Germans are detouring their divisions towards the Somme, that Rotterdam and France have fallen, and that France and Germany have signed an armistice. Is this possible?*

Our news seems to take forever, and the static of the shortwave radio makes it maddening to listen to. The early morning dispatches here tell what has been going on in Europe all day, but the day-to-day reports give little sense about the larger story. I don't suppose it is any different for you in Santiago or Valparaiso, but do write to tell us what you hear.

As ever, we rely on the Americans to give us up-to-date news but, sometimes, they do no better, or our encounters center on picking up the children from school and we exercise the 'pas devant' rule; no one likes to talk about the war in front of them. Fortunately, the girls are not interested in reading the papers even if we mistakenly leave one in view.

The only place they can't escape the news is when we go to the movies and the Movietone newsreels show us soldiers falling in battle, airplanes buzzing around like flies in the sky, bombs exploding, and the lines of refugees fleeing along avenues lined with poplars, as if the people are going on a picnic with a special lot of provisions. None of it seems to have any more significance than the cartoons the girls watch right after. Bugs Bunny and Elmer Fudd blast away at each other, fall down and get up to no ill effect, and the classical soundtrack is as beautiful and familiar to the girls as if I were playing it on the piano, or as if they were hearing it on our records at home.

Benny and I are mute on the subject of war. How could we answer their questions? We read that, steps away from Brazil, Nazi activities are increasing in Uruguay and that the US Secretary of State, Cordell Hull, thinks it is even worse that they are indifferent or apathetic to the Nazi presence. Clearly the United States is not blind to what is happening to the Jews in Europe. Is it possible Jews are required to register in the Netherlands now? With all the Germans in Argentina, Uruguay, Chile and southern Brazil, will the venom to Jews spread here, too?

On a local level, and in welcomed relief, the newspaper runs the results of the horse races at the Jockey Club Brasileiro, charts the phases of the moon, the scores of regattas, soccer games, water polo and chess tournaments. In large print, they announce that Toscanini is conducting Tschaikowsky's Romeo and Juliet and his Fifth Symphony at Rio's Teatro Municipal. The big movie houses are starring Bette Davis and Errol Flynn in The Private Lives of Elizabeth and Essex, and Greta Garbo seduces Melvin Douglas while poking fun at the Soviet Regime in Ninotchka, none of which Benny and I attend.

I hope you can read this cramped writing. I am out of the clear onion skin and am splurging on this blue variety. I'm also indulging in paragraphs to favor your eyes.

Abrazos, Queta

* * *

1940. São Paulo.

I am three. Our parents moved here last year from Rio, where I was born. Brazil has not entered the war my mother tells me her knitting goes to. I don't understand. I am in a nursery with a mix of English, French, American and Brazilian children when the practice air raids sound. We are well-behaved, obey our teachers' Portuguese drill commands, walk quickly to the stairs leading to a basement that has been prepared for possible long stays there. I like going down the stairs one foot at a time while I hold onto a wood banister that feels silky. I have a mat of my own that has been rolled out for me on the cool concrete floor. I lie on it quietly next to my nursery schoolmates. We are close to the shelves stocked with school supplies and bandages. I am glad we are not permitted to talk to one another because I seldom want to speak. Perhaps I am not sure what language to use; at home we speak French, in school we speak Portuguese. The all-clear signal means the end of what the teachers call our nap time. I leave my mat for someone else to roll up, line up at the stairs, reach for the banister and return upwards to the heat of the classroom and schoolyard to teasing, chases, pushing, scraped knees, "He did," "She did," tears. The war rehearsal is better. It's peaceful. I like silence.

In São Paulo, we live in a white stucco house with a red tiled roof, which I love. In the back garden, my mother has built a playhouse the size my two and a half year older sister, Arlette, and I can step into with ease but grown-ups cannot. The playhouse is white with green shutters. Mummy has planted forget-me-nots around the playhouse and, if we feel like staying inside it in the shade, we can pick the small blue flowers just by leaning outside the low windows. Better than staying inside either house, however, is chasing Arlette in the yard to bite her. I don't really sink my teeth in, but I want to hold her arm still so I can inhale the sun on her skin the way I inhale the sun on mine. The scent of sweat, saliva and sun is a pleasure I risk repeated punishments for. Arlette is blue-eyed and has blond curls and looks like Shirley Temple. "We could eat her up!" friends and strangers exclaim. "She is sunshine," they say. I need to taste for myself.

My mother scolds me but Arlette knows how to get even. She tells me the worms we stir up in the children's pan of mud and water we've mixed in the garden are spaghetti. "Eat them," she says, and I do. "Go on. Put your foot in the pinico," she says taunting me towards the chamber pot we have peed in overnight. I do and we both laugh until I have to pee again. Arlette's punishments are tricks I don't mind because I want to win her approval, and because to laugh is the best thing of all, and Arlette brings laughter.

She also brings me protection. Our mother is never reluctant to scold or to give us a smart slap on the behind when we misbehave but, one day, Mummy tells us that what we have done is so bad (might we have neglected some war drill?), she is going to leave the spanking up to our father. Neither she nor he has done this before. That night, already bathed and in our pajamas, we listen for our father's shoe steps down the tiled hall.

"Quick," Arlette orders. She thrusts a large thin Babar book at me. I watch as she stuffs another rectangular volume down the back of her pajama bottoms and I copy her just as Daddy walks in. It does not take him long to guess who was clever enough to trick him, and he bursts out laughing until tears of relief roll down his cheeks. He kisses us goodnight without a question.

It is in our home in São Paulo where we first practice against night-time air raids by covering windows so enemy pilots will not know a town is beneath them. I hear the bellowing arc of the air raid sirens rise and fall, sing the notes back to myself, chin up for the high notes, chin down for the low ones. I marvel at the searchlights swooping across the sky and crisscrossing through each other soundlessly. Will they spot a plane? What happens if they do? Our mother runs to the windows with blankets she somehow fastens and tucks in at window corners. She turns out all the lights and allows a candle or two to flicker. We have to be quiet to listen for practice planes and to the radio, which we have put on low for any kind of news. Arlette and I can't fight. Nice.

In 1941 Otis moves our family back to Rio.

CHAPTER THREE

Which Side?

July, 1941—Rio

Querida familia,

The lack of familial news from France dims every thought and colors our imaginations. Humor me, please. I think how matters of chance play into our lives. Papa was asked to come to Santiago for a two year-trial run to work for La Casa Prat. If he hadn't fallen so in love with Chile, our own family would have gone back to France and stayed there, and we'd have been in the middle of two world wars.

Here in Rio it feels as if we still are settling from our return from São Paulo. Nega, the Italian orphan I found wandering around outside our house on Presidente Prudente, has come with us. The girls love her, as do I. Though she never mentions her parents, she learned from someone how to make the best pasta in the world. She rolls out the dough, then slices it into strands of linguine which she drapes to dry over the railings on the front porch. It's a cheerful sight and makes our mouths water in anticipation. A handsome green-eyed Indian called Agenor keeps our wood floors clean and sparkling, a treat to walk on barefoot in the heat. Denise insists on calling him Argentão because his hair is silver, argento, in Portuguese. Good thing he's proud of it.

Benny, as is his wont, has made friends with everyone, has new golfing and tennis companions, many Brazilians, not just ex-pats. I never know where we fit into the mix, but the mix is so big and varied, it doesn't seem to matter much.

At heart, I am overwhelmed to know war news—real news. I am susceptible to gossip. Do you remember that Brazil's President, Getulio Vargas's son, Lutero, married a German, Ingeborg ten Haeff from Dusseldorf last year? She is a musician/singer, but who knows where her allegiances lie and how they play on papa-in-law. Even this weighs heavily with me as we wonder which side Brazil will take in this war.

Bits and pieces: we heard that in January, the United States denied a Vichy French request to welcome Jewish German refugees to its shores, and that in February, the Nazis in Austria started a plan to send Jews to the Polish ghettos. We learned about the Lend-lease bill the United States Congress approved in March, so I guess Britain and the Free French will be better able to protect themselves with American armaments.

The year has started off terribly with Britain losing carriers in the Mediterranean. At least the Brits sunk the Bismarck last month. I don't know why I feel obliged to tell you what must be in your news, too, but I feel isolated and I need some confirmation. There are too many rumors, too many censors of anything going between Europe and the western hemisphere, too many subs hidden in the oceans, too much of an overarching threat to civilization.

Adjusting to tropical storms and plugged pipes and lugging water from a well keep me on my toes when Arlette and Denise aren't a full-time occupation.

Queta.

* * *

Today, we had one of the wonderful rain storms. We heard it coming from the sound of the palmeiras slapping by the beach, and from the storm moving into our block. The sky looked pocked and purple like ripe guava skins, and the smell of the air was salty and green. When the rain starts it feels as if it stops your nose and shuts your eyes, and then the water starts running in the gutter on the street and, at first, the heat of the street warms the water. If Mummy lets us, we can go in our *tamancos* to play in the water outside the house and watch it rise up over our feet and ankles until the water feels cold. I like it when the rains come and go fast and you can see the clouds taking the rain in a clump out to sea, or up into the mountains. But if the rain lasts and lasts, the fresh smell goes away and everything smells of mold. It collects stinky and black in the corners of windows and doors outside, in towels or shower curtains and lasts until the dry heat comes to cook it, and then it disappears. During the wet times, Mummy keeps a light on inside the piano and in our closets to keep them as dry as possible.

What I don't like about rains storms is that we have to go get water from a well in back of the house. It seems funny that we have water shortages from the tap when we have all this water falling from the skies, but Mummy says it's because the sewer and pipe lines are broken. Nega and Argentão come with big buckets. Mummy gives us small ones, and we help carry the water to the second floor. The awful job is Argentão's because he is the strongest one here. He has to move the heavy cement lid off the well and when he does, hundreds of *bichos* scurry and fly out so that we have to duck and cover our faces and arms. Mummy tries to make us concentrate on some of the prettier and slower bugs that stay behind. "Look, how delicate they are, almost transparent, skinny-legged and, they walk on water!" I know she is trying to make us feel better because she doesn't like bugs either.

Mummy took us to the Botanical Gardens up in the mountains last week. There's quicksand there. It looks grey and ugly and I am scared of it. Mummy tells us cats and monkeys can get caught in it and drown, but if we hold onto her hand all the time, we won't step in it. She even makes us look up by telling us to see how bright the red and green and blue macaws and parrots are. And then she tells us to look into the distance to Guanabara Bay to see if we can spot a submarine's periscope. We are not scared of any subs because the Brazilians strung a huge net across the entrance to the bay to keep them from getting closer to shore.

The explorers who discovered the bay thought it was a river, um rio, Mummy says in her voice that tells me her thoughts are far, far away, but then it strikes me for the first time that is the reason our city is called Rio. The 'of January,' de Janeiro, doesn't seem as important. People rarely use it. *Where do you live?* they ask. *Rio* says it all.

River or bay, we never spot any submarines.

At night, I dream I step into quicksand and can't make my legs move.

CHAPTER FOUR

Brazil Enters the War

El 28 de agosto, 1942

Queridos,

Now we're in it. This time we got the news from many sources: the radio, our American friends at Otis, Esso execs, The National City Bank, the different Embassies. Today we saw a copy of The New York Times from Saturday, August 22, 1942. I copy it for you here: "Rio de Janeiro, Brazil, Aug. 21 (AP)—The War Minister General Enrico Gaspar Dutra today issued a proclamation stressing the gravity of Brazil's situation and declaring the army was ready to repel aggressions of those who 'using criminal methods' destroyed Brazilian life, sinking harmless coastwise ships in the Brazilian seas."

Last week, Brazil lost six ships to German U-boats, and then American airmen sunk the U-boats. What are your newspapers saying and how are you reacting to the news? Love, Queta

P.S. Benny just came in with The New York Times of Sunday, August 23. It reads: "Brazil declares war on Axis; Nazis force Don bend crossing; US submarines bag four in the Pacific." They say that just before war was declared, there was an incident on the steps of Rio's Municipal Theater when someone lit a Nazi flag afire. Good, says I. Brazil is the first nation in South America to enter the war, so we are considered a new ally in the fight, but we have not included Japan in the Declaration of Belligerency— too many Japanese here already running the agriculture. We also don't want to put our western neighbors in harm's way, which means you, my dear Chilenos, Peruanos, and northwards. Besos, Queta

Another P.S. Here's an anecdote that may not have come to you and will give you another view of the Brazilian's siding with the Allies. One story centers around the sailing of the Queen Mary (the Grey Ghost, as she is being called now that she is in battleship grey, including the smokestacks) full of American troops en route to North Africa to help stop Rommel's advances.

We have a friend who was watching from the building A Noite—The Night, named after the newspaper it houses and publishes. It is Rio's first skyscraper of twenty floors (Otis elevators installed, of course) with a fine view of the Mauá docks and harbor. Unbeknownst to our friend, his son was on that boat.

Rumor had it that the German subs were in the harbor waiting to sink the ship, and everyone was nervous about what the reaction of the Brazilians would be; after all, the general view among Brazilians themselves is that the country does better with an authority figure (read dictator?). Our current president Vargas certainly is one. Hitler's decisiveness appeals to him and to a lot of people here, in a "that's what we need," kind of thinking.

The Brazilian sense of inferiority is not helped by the fact that all the big banks, industrial companies, phones, light and power and transport are owned and run by foreigners. A few of the nastier types call Brazilians "Brazis" behind their backs.

Anyway, the usual procedure when a ship leaves is that it is pulled beyond the mouth of the harbor slowly by tugs so as not to create waves for the smaller boats around—and there are lots of them. After that, it can fire its engines. Everyone watching noticed the Queen Mary did not wait for tugs but fired herself up close to her possible 28 knots, plowed out of the harbor and continued in a running zig-zag, small boats and torpedoes be damned. She made it.

The underlying thought among many was what if the Queen Mary *had been torpedoed? Would the Brazilians have seen this as another success for the Axis and gone to their side? After all, the news of the Axis advances in Europe and North Africa has been uniquely about its military successes, and the dictatorial allure that Hitler holds for Vargas has made us quake. You can imagine our relief to hear Brazil declare itself on the side of the Allies. Pearl Harbor seems more than 8 months ago.*

Queta.

* * *

I don't know why our father chose golf for Arlette and tennis for me, but I'm glad he did. Arlette has to take golf lessons in Gavea, but I can take tennis at the Rio Country Club, which is much nearer. I love my teacher who is an Indian and whose bones seem as fragile as a bird's, but he is strong and jumps as if he were taking wing. His name is Aguero and he looks like Argentão with his green eyes. He's not much taller than I am and we are always glad to see one another. He and I never tire of hitting balls to each other, even in the heat. He is teaching me to serve.

Mr. Reis is our swimming teacher, and I think he is wonderful, too. Arlette's friend, Sally, also takes lessons from him with Arlette and me at the Club but I think Mr. Reis gets annoyed with us because we laugh so much. We play "I'll save you," and nearly drown laughing. He makes us do stretching exercises before we get into the pool. Sally and Arlette are good at the breast stroke but I can't get the kick. Mine keeps going sideways. I am faster than both of them at the backstroke. "That's your stroke, Denise," he tells me over and over and encourages me to swim as fast as I can. It's easy because I don't have my head in the water. I also like the crawl. I pretend I'm stretching for something important that always keeps just out of my reach so I have to keep going.

We can walk on the Club House grounds two ways. One is the

wide walk that goes to the pool and by the front sides of the tennis courts. The second way is through a small back path that is very shaded with ferns and trees and feels as if it's wet all the time. I see rats here sometimes. Mummy doesn't like us to use that path, but not because of the rats. "No one can see you if you get into trouble," she says. I think she is afraid a waiter will come out and tease us or something, but if I go by the dark, narrow path, I can come right to where the three-toed sloth hangs upside down from the branch of one of the big fig trees. I can stand there for a long time, talk or hum to him, and he never moves. His nails are really long and would scratch, I think. Sometimes I can smell the stink bugs here. You can smell them before you see them and should get out of their way before they sting you.

I like getting home to our maid, Raimunda.

CHAPTER FIVE

War News

Le 30 août, 1942

Bien chère Margot,

How are you? Are you still making noises about going to Paris? Surely no one will grant you passage these days, though I appreciate you must be impatient. You will see your city of hopes one day. Maybe I am the only other sibling who wants to go as much as you. I'm memorizing maps so we can walk the streets together when we meet on the Left Bank. This is definitely not a time to be in Paris.

Through always secret sources, we know Benny's sister, Jacqueline, and their mother are not having a good time with the Boches in their apartment on Théodore de Banville. They show the women sausages and chocolate they have bought, then eat it all in front of them and offer them nothing. Jacqueline is young and pretty. What will the soldiers do to her?

I'm copying a portion of a story left over from another page of the August 22nd New York Times almost exactly a year ago. One of these days, I will tell you how this kind of news affected us (and how my secretarial skills honed in Santiago's First National City Bank helped!), but I am paranoid about censors.

"Brazilian police today continued their search for secret radio transmitters which they believe were used to send out information

*resulting in the torpedoing and sinking of five coastal steamers and a
schooner with the loss of about 600 lives."*

*The newspaper Diario da Noite said that "the fifth transmitter seized
in five days was found in the possession of Adler Becker, a German
mechanic employed by the electrical goods firm of Siemens Schickert. He
was arrested."*

Bisous à tous, Queta

* * *

Our home in Rio stretches the length of the middle floor of a
three-floor apartment building in Ipanema, one block away from
the beach. The Brazilian man and wife, who live on the first floor,
have no children, so we don't see them very often. The wife's
gold bracelets clank when she pinches our cheeks, the way all
Brazilians do, and she calls us 'bemzinhas' little dears. I cozy up
to her perfume and deep colors of lipstick and suits. An American
couple lives on the top floor with their three small boys. Mummy
loves to speak English to Lydia, the young mother, but the boys
are pests. "You ought to throw a bucket of cold water on that one,"
Mummy tells the mother when her son is having a tantrum. Our
mother has never done that to us yet, but I am given more reason
to behave. Her voice carries weight; I see Lydia slosh her son.

Our living space starts with a large covered balcony in the front
facing the street, and ends with the kitchen, the maids' quarters,
and another smaller balcony. Here the cook kills the chickens and
drinks their blood, the laundress washes clothes, towels and
sheets, the floor man keeps his waxes and cloths, and everyone
helps filter bugs from the well water. In between are the living
room, dining room, three bedrooms, a huge bathroom where we
wander in and out of each other's showers, and a space we call the
copa, a tiled-floor pantry. In our house, we fill the *copa* with tall

forget-me-not-blue drop-leaf desks for Arlette and me, and a work table for our mother. The single telephone, which we are not allowed to use, sits on her table. Our bedrooms look out onto the long driveway that runs from the gate at the sidewalk entrance to a garage in back and over which there is a small apartment.

I have never seen it used until the day a European couple moves in. Since it is rare to have any cars come into the drive, Arlette and I glue ourselves to our window ledge to find out what is going on. We are semi-shaded by a wooden blind that rolls down a frame we can pull in close to the wall or push out. Out is better to catch the breezes. From where we lean, we know the couple is European because of their shoes. In Brazil, most people wear sandals or *tamancos*, wooden-soled open-toed clogs. Americans come in loafers, spectator pumps, wing-tipped cordovans and saddle shoes, shoes we see in the Esther Williams movies, shoes we wish we had for ourselves. Other ex-pat women, including our mother, wear high-heeled sandals or pumps cut high on the instep. Silk stockings are hard, if not impossible, to get, yet few ex-pat women go bare-legged.

This woman has on stockings with a seam in back and black stocky-heeled, worn lace-up shoes. The man, too, wears scuffed lace-ups that look as if they started out brown. Both have on full-length coats as if they have left cold weather and not bothered to change for the Rio heat. Both wear dark hats, hers a crumpled bunch of felt with a veil drawn back over it, his a fedora like the men wear in the movies. To us they look middle-aged, in their thirties. We watch them get out from a black sedan and walk up the outside stairs to their new home without looking around to notice the fig or papaya trees, or the parakeets or children who might be around to wave hello to. They carry a small brown suitcase apiece and the chauffeur brings up a black cube-shaped leather carrier that seems to be heavy. Arlette and I seldom see them come out of the apartment but sometimes at night, we hear them walk down the driveway and whine the gate shut in back of them.

We begin to hear clicks at night coming from their apartment. I don't know when Arlette and I first notice these sounds. Maybe it is the scent of the night-blooming cereus that grows along the wall of the house on the other side of the driveway that wakes us the first time. The flower doesn't bloom often but, when it does, its scent is as strong as a stink bug's. Instead of avoiding this scent, however, we run to the window to gulp in its perfume and to wonder at the stark white flower we can see no matter how dark the night. Arlette and I pay no attention to the clicking, but our mother does.

Night after night, with her secretarial skills of taking dictation rapidly, she transcribes the Morse Code coming from the apartment. I see these pages in the morning by the window in her bedroom, and watch the pages grow over a few days. I peek at the dots and dashes and her shorthand squiggles beside them. They make no sense to me and I wonder for a moment if she is writing a music notation I have never seen. After she sees me examine one page, she secretes the rest of her work. Clearly this is not Arlette's or my business, more material for the 'pas devant' rule. Typically, I don't ask.

What Mummy recognizes is that the transcripts of the letters make sense in German. She writes the translation in German next to the code, translates it into English, and somehow gets the code and the German and English translations to the American Embassy.

Arlette and I don't learn any of these details. We have no idea our mother understands German, a language she would not have been willing to admit to speaking during the war. We learn years later it is a language she picked up by doing work for a German professor at Oberlin.

I remember the day the police come as well as the day the couple arrived a few months before. The police car draws up alongside the garage, two officers go upstairs, knock on the door, and then we hear upset voices inside. When the couple comes down the outside stairs, they are in full view wearing handcuffs like in the Movietone news.

"Mummy, why have the police come? What did those people do?"

"They were putting people's lives in danger," she says.

CHAPTER SIX

Rituals

December, 1942

Queridos todos,

    Tales and rumors fly. I heard via a friend of a friend of a friend . . . these tales reach us like ripples from skipping stones until they slowly fade, and yet may be our most reliable sources . . . about 3,500 young Brazilians recruited from the interior who were taken in a train whose windows had been blacked out. They traveled for two days and got off at an (unstated) seaport where they were put on board a ship bound for North Africa to help General Montgomery. All were violently seasick and terrified especially when they landed first in Naples and people began spitting on them. Apparently, their uniforms looked like German ones, and the local population is none too happy with the Germans.

    In the meantime, I have to laugh at my days of important trivia: delousing the new cook—and therefore everyone else, too, a matter of egalitarianism as much as preventive care; teaching new recipes; looking after the floor-man's wife whose gums are infected; putting down hems in Arlette's dresses, turning them up for Denise's; teaching the girls to sew, Arlette to play piano. Denise wants to play Chopin immediately, so I told her I would not teach her. She was furious. She is serious, headstrong but zany, too. Loves to dance and constantly is humming music I play, or singing Carnival songs even if she has heard them only once. Arlette is sunny always, her blond curls a corolla of warm light.

Amazing. Good sense of humor. I hear her laughing with Benny. Both see the absurd side of things. I must go exchange ration cards for sugar. Denise is coming with me, so I will finish this later . . .

* * *

Our mothers chatter in French, Spanish, Portuguese and English when they go to roll bandages to send to the front at the stuffy Red Cross center in Rio. I don't know what 'the front' means, but I know the bandages are for soldiers who get hurt. It also means we knit a lot because "It's cold where the soldiers are." It got cold here once. The temperature went down to 50 degrees and we were so cold, we had to borrow coats from our American friends for a week. Mummy tells us that where the soldiers are, they have to keep on their sweaters and scarves and jackets for months. Arlette and I knit and purl short squares or long scarves.

We have rations. We line up with food coupons for corn meal, flour and sugar, for example. The exchange of a coupon for a bag of almost anything makes the transaction seem important. The cruzeiro bills in Rio are often tattered and filthy—"Go wash your hands, Denise. That bill was probably in a leper's hands two minutes ago"—but the coupons are crisp and belong only to us.

At a school raffle, I win a box of *Maizena*, corn meal. I am disappointed and wonder why the grown-ups congratulate me for being a lucky girl. What will I do with corn meal except give it up to the cook?

What I like is to line up. When I am not in school, my mother takes me with her and I have her all to myself. We advance slowly on the sidewalk in front of the different stores, in and out of the shade of mango trees that shed their leaves, and of giant ficus trees that drop their small, round figlets. I have plenty to crunch with my white sandals in happy assurance of their unending supply as we pass from tree to tree. In line, Mummy stands silently, but the flowers on her dress look as if they have taken life from the moving shadows of the tree leaves above us. When she does speak, her voice is a susurrus of 's'es, a sibilance on an intaken 'yes'.

There is seldom enough time in our progress to sit on the occasional bench. Mummy hates the heat. To pass the time, she moves her fingers in the palm of my hand so I can guess which piano pieces she is practicing. By their rhythms, I guess Chopin mazurkas or Beethoven études, or sometimes the Stephen Foster songs she has picked up somewhere and that I hear her play at home. In my mind, I sing back the music she is playing into my palm. This war effort of standing in line satisfies me completely.

CHAPTER SEVEN

Queta

January, 1943

¡Holá! mi familia,

. . . I take up where I left off. Thanks for your notes. I do not show them to the girls. I know I should, but we are so scared to have them ask us about Benny's family, that we don't speak of any family at all—a sad consequence. I love our girls. How will they look back on our silence?

Little by little, I infer we are not alone in our reservations about sharing family news. The many accents in town hide secrets from Italy, Hungary, Russia, Romania and Germany. It is hard for our few German friends who have been in South America for ages. No one trusts anyone on the side of the Axis.

With the world so hungry for oil, rumors—always rumors—have it that Ploesti in Romania supplies the Germans with a third of its war needs and that the Allies are plotting to bomb it. The physical mess this war leaves behind is something we cannot imagine, still less the psychological destruction.

And now I relieve you of dark realities as I have to leave again for a light one: teacher conferences at the girls' school which, in contrast to everything else—and even in and of themselves—are pretty amusing. I will mail this anyway. I hope this finds you all well. We are.

Love, Queta

* * *

According to her passport, my mother's name, now that she is married to my father, is Enriqueta Marguerite Bottin Benzacar, but everyone calls her "Queta." She is 5'2" and has blue eyes. I know her eyes are blue because I look into them a lot but I have not thought about measuring her. Looking at her passport makes me feel grown-up. I see it once when it tumbles out of her jewelry box and she treats it as casually as she does her jewelry. I must have been sick, playing the princess-in-a-castle game she invented for Arlette and me. During the day, she invites us into the big double bed she and our father sleep in and arranges pillows in back, in front and on our sides so that nothing escapes our cushioned fort; then, she gives us her jewelry box to explore.

The box is a darkly-lacquered rectangle. It is not the outside that interests me but the scarlet velvet lining of the compartments inside, and the construction: I can lift the first layer out like a tray to discover a second layer of smaller compartments below. I never dump the contents of the box into my sanctuary because there are not many pieces and each piece shines in a different light. Next to her own aquamarine ring, Mummy keeps two others that our godparents have given Arlette and me. The stones are much smaller but the settings make them seem like copies of her own. She has some ruby earrings with little diamonds on the outside, but the stones pale in comparison to her pearl necklace which I like to thread lightly through my fingers. The pearls stay smooth and the same temperature even when my fingers seem hot and sticky.

I never misplace so much as an earring and appreciate her carefully-planned game; I often am sick with stomach problems of one sort or another, reactions to bug bites—a spider's bite on the calf keeps me in bed in a darkened room for three days—and, once, with a concussion from getting hit on the head with a baseball hit by an American boy I had a crush on. I forgave him but I didn't like him after that. We also get to recover from chicken pox, mumps, and measles in our parents' bed. My parents know I am well when I start to ask for my favorite foods: cheese soufflé and fresh figs.

Mummy often plays the piano. She says she doesn't like Bach, but she likes Beethoven and Mozart and American songs she learned in Oberlin. She teaches Arlette still, but not me anymore. She says I am too impatient. She really got mad at me once in São Paulo when we were going to see a ballet dancer, Geneviève Moulin, who dances with the Ballets Russes de Monte Carlo. They had come to dance for the Paulistas. Mummy knows Geneviève from Santiago because Geneviève's family lived there. Geneviève's sister had polio and Mummy used to sit for her. Geneviève was scared of getting it, but didn't, which is good because she's a dancer.

Mummy made me take a nap so I would be wide awake for the ballet performance. I was already four and I hated to take naps. When Mummy woke me, I woke up sweaty and really cross because she had interrupted a nice dream. When we got to the bus stop three blocks away, she shouted at me: "If you don't stop complaining, you can go home all by yourself. I don't want your company! You are ruining the afternoon and I don't want you to ruin the ballet."

The thought that I might miss the ballet made me keep quiet and I'm glad I went. We saw 'Swan Lake' and after the performance, we got to meet Geneviève backstage. Her eyes were so full of make-up, they looked black, but when I saw her from the audience, her eyes looked normal. She and Mummy were so glad to see each other!

I don't remember what Mummy talks to me about most of the time. When I am with her, it is as if I absorb whatever she is thinking through her hands. Maybe it's because I'm not sure in which language our mother speaks to me and I don't pay attention. At home, our parents speak French to Arlette and to me, the language of their own parents, but Mummy also speaks to me in Spanish, the language of Chile, where she was born and where she grew up with her five siblings after her parents sailed over from France. How else would I have learned the Spanish I know? When she braids my hair in the morning, it's *Hijita, ¡por diós!* I hear her scold at my squirming, not B*on Dieu, tiens-toi tranquille!* Our lullabies are in Spanish.

Los pollitos dicen, pío, pío, pío,	The chicks cheep *pío, pío, pío*
Cuando tienen hambre,	When they are hungry,
Cuando tienen frío.	When they are cold.
La gallina busca el maíz y el trigo	The hen brings corn and wheat
Y abre sus alas	And opens her wings
Para dar abrigo.	To give shelter.
Señora Sant'Ana,	Our Lady, Saint Ana,
Carita de luna,	With the face of the moon,
Neste, neste nido,	In this nest,
Que tiene la cuna.	Lies the cradle.

But when the war and the Americans come pouring into Rio, other languages scuttle into dark holes like sand crabs afraid to be identified. Arlette and I learn English and use it with complete focus. *Pourquoi tu ne me responds plus en français?* my father asks with hurt in his voice. Our mother never questions why we no longer answer her in French; she also has switched to English. Mummy loves English as much as she loves French, and she loves the United States.

We find this out after the victory in Europe is announced and we sense that travel on the seas will be open for more than the military. Our mother does two surprising things. First, she places what we know is a complicated and expensive call to make from Rio to someone called Angie Sands in Skaneateles, New York. "She was my roommate at college," Mummy explains, as if I understand what college is.

"We're going to go see her," is the second unsettling decision. Mummy delivers it in a voice so quiet, calm and sure, she makes it sound like a reprieve from dying.

I think of the anthem words that promise everlasting life. I heard them in church when Arlette and I went with Wendy and Eric Wilson. The minister said if we ate the body of Christ and drank his blood, that's what we'd get, everlasting life, and that we wouldn't have to die. The minister came around offering the wafers that were supposed to be the body of Christ and Eric said "No, thanks." Arlette and I didn't take the wafers either, but we didn't say thank you. And then we had awful giggles and had to leave the church because the grown-ups were giving us bad looks. We did not tell Mummy or Daddy, although Daddy would have laughed.

But now, when I hear Mummy make the phone call to the United States and say she is going to see a friend of hers there that Daddy, Arlette and I don't know, I feel excluded and uneasy. It makes me realize two things: that the idea of going to see her friend from Oberlin College must have been first on a when-the-war-ends wish list she and my father have talked about, and that she might have had a life she liked better than the one she is living in Brazil. This second thought makes me feel terrible. I thought she was happy here.

In the meantime, our mothers knit on and teach us how to manage the needles and wools, some of them scratchy, others not. Everyone knits, even our eye doctor, Dr. Neureuter, knits when he is with his patients and when he answers the phone in fourteen different languages. It doesn't matter that he is German because he has lived in Rio for many years before the war, and he is nice and makes everyone laugh. The billowing wools fill up his lap like clouds in dark and bright colors. Arlette takes to knitting, but I don't. She knows I am bored and not very handy. "Let's read the Bible while we do this," Arlette suggests one day. I'm not sure if our visit to Sunday School with our friends put this idea into her head, but we never get beyond Genesis and my knitted squares stop during the begats.

And then, Mummy does something special with her knitting. She gets the idea when she hears a stranger on the street say about Arlette's blue eyes and blond hair that she is *uma Alemãnzinha*—a German child.

Our mother knits a sweater for Arlette with the French blue, white and red colors, a white lily, on the front, a rooster on the back. These are well-known emblems during the war, the Fleur de Lis the French flower, the rooster a symbol for Charles de Gaulle. It must be horribly hot for Arlette to wear that sweater, but our mother will not allow any chance of Arlette's being in any way identified as a German. I do not think of her sweater in terms of political artwork then, but that is what the sweater turns out to be.

It is while knitting that our mother tells us stories of how she misbehaved in class in Chile, how she got her friends to join her tapping their feet very quickly under the desks until they teased the nuns into thinking there was an earthquake happening. I like my mother's mischief. I want to hear more, but she speaks little to me as if her mind is far away on the music she moves her fingers to, or on things I don't know about. We grow up freely but politely and don't break the boundaries. There are clear ranges of conversation, the first the adults let children in on, the second only for adults. Mummy does not confuse the two.

CHAPTER EIGHT

Benny

February, 1943

Queridos,

It seems only days ago that we were celebrating Christmas and the girls were yelling out the side balcony "Merci Papa Noël" for the small gifts we give them. The patent leather Mary Jane shoes were the definite hit, but shoes always are for these two. I sometimes think they recognize people by their footwear rather than their faces. American shoes signal heaven.

Arlette came home with some problems in Portuguese spelling the other day. Our President, canny creature that he is, is a nationalist (Yes, hang on, her Portuguese and his nationalism do have a connection!).

Vargas understood that one way to incorporate the increasing immigrant groups in Brazil early on in his reign was to obligate the teaching and use of Portuguese as a way of cutting ties to countries of origin. He thought, however, that the old orthography needed revamping so he, himself—Getulio-style—created the new spellings.

Trouble is that sometimes, especially in our ex-pat schools, the books we have at hand contain the old orthography. Arlette was dutifully learning from one of those readers when the teacher brought her—and her fellow pupils—up short. "Wrong," said she. "Revise!"

Since they all are in the early stages of reading and spelling the language, there was some consternation. Doesn't help that we all prefer the old spelling, so we joke about having a richness of choices and encourage Arlette to spell phonetically. Isn't 'x' a prettier way of saying 'ch' which sounds like 'sh' in any case? She will get good grades regardless.

Benny joined the French League here. There is less doubt of news that comes through them. He remains tight-lipped at home, puts on the radio to the opera hour, or to whatever classical music he can find, and plays and sings with the girls. I watched him demonstrate to Denise about how opera singers have to shape their mouths to mold the sounds they want you to understand. Denise was transfixed but her nose was crinkled as if she didn't like having to watch her father's mouth moving so oddly up close. Benny, of course, did not tell her that the reason he is so versed in this is that he used to spend hours watching his own mother practice different opera roles, a fantasy of hers.

I have gathered the real reason Benny's mother divorced his father was that she couldn't stand to be tethered to a man much older than she, especially one who didn't give a tuppence (as our English friends around here say) about her passion to follow a singing career. To show him she was serious, she abandoned the children to their lawyer father and fled home solo to Paris, where she stayed. Benny was seven, one sister eight, the other five. Hints allow as to how they hated their soon-to-be stepmother. What a dreadful life, yet they made fun for themselves, even if unorthodox.

The one story I have heard Benny tell our girls about is when he and his sisters had to walk across a big park to get to school. If one of them had to pee en route, he would tell them to go ahead. "I'll sing the Marseillaise," he'd say, "and that way people will pay attention to me, not to you." Their stressed bladders welcomed the ruse and the Marseillaise lives on in our household with every visit to the loo.

You mentioned father's chrysanthemums give him pleasure every fall. Tell me what each of you is pursuing? Is Maman playing the piano much? Anybody with arthritis yet? Any budding tennis players among the youngest generation? How are the horses? Who's riding them?

I imagine, especially with Chile remaining neutral in the war, no one speaks much about politics, except within small circles. We tend to be in a waiting mode, though for what first, I scarcely dare imagine. Teetering times.

Love from your chief teeterer, Queta

* * *

These are the things I know or think to ask about our father. He has four names: Henri Charles Jean Benzacar. He has dark hair and dark eyes. He was born in Bordeaux, France in 1900, a year that makes it easy for me to figure out how old he is. When he left France after the First World War, he sailed for New York City, where he met an American friend he worked with in the ambulance service during the war. Daddy said it was very muddy all the time in the war, and that he and his friend decided they needed to change socks when they threw them against the sides of the tent and they stuck. This was one of the few stories Daddy liked to tell about himself. It made him laugh. Me, too.

My father also told me he didn't know what to do when he got to New York, but his Army friend said: "Otis Elevator Company trains engineers in Yonkers. It isn't far from here. You have an engineer's degree. Why don't you go train with them? It will give you six months to see if you like it, and you can work on that terrible English of yours."

He said he ended up liking the work in Yonkers, a thriving town by the Hudson, an attractive place to be. He stayed with Otis. They sent him to Chicago, Havana, Buenos Aires, and Santiago, cities experiencing an increase of buildings over five stories high. Those needed elevators. It meant Otis had to edge out Schindler, their only real competition, in my father's opinion, and Daddy liked the challenge. He thought Otis made a fine product.

In Santiago he met and married Mummy. They moved with Otis to Brazil. They had Arlette in São Paulo, me in Rio. Like our mother, our father speaks French, Spanish, Portuguese, English, but he really is most comfortable in French.

I know he has a younger sister, Gilberte, because we met Uncle Andrew, her husband, during the war. A photograph of Dinah, Daddy's older sister, sits in a corner over our couch in Rio. She is a beautiful gypsy-like woman with her dark thick curls, dark eyes.

Everything about my father is joyful and private. Everyone calls him "Benny," short for Benzacar. He doesn't scold, but on two points he is clear: "Don't talk about money, politics or religion—*pas poli*—not polite." The second is: "Keep hold of your papers and never lose your passport." Because he speaks to us seriously so seldom, I pay close attention. His reaction to questions he does not wish to answer is deflection.

Fous-moi le camp!—Go away!" He laughs and calls us by his nicknames based on our initials, 'AMBétante' for Arlette Marguerite Benzacar, 'DEButante' for Denise Emma Benzacar. I'm sure Arlette never is hurt to be called annoying as she so clearly is the sunny, fun child—fun for our parents, fun for me. Or he brings out a pencil and paper and draws in his magnificent engineer's doodlings the figure of a man sitting on a chair and leaning his hands on an umbrella in front of him, then hands it to us and says "Here! Tell me what he is waiting for." Or he starts singing one of the many French children's songs he knows.

Promenons nous dans les bois,	Let's go walking in the woods
Pendant que le loup n'y est pas.	While the wolf isn't there.
Où est-tu?	Where are you?
Que fais-tu?	What are you doing?
Entends-tu?	Are you listening?

Our father sings many verses and answers the song's repeated questions of where the wolf is and what he is doing in a deep scary voice. He tells us how many items of clothing the wolf still has to put on before he catches up to us in the woods.

Je mets mes culottes . . . Je mets mes pantalons . . . je mets ma chemise . . . Je mets ma cravatte . . . Je mets ma ceinture . . . Je mets mon chapeau.

I'm putting on my shorts . . . I'm putting on my trousers . . . I'm putting on my shirt . . . I'm tying my tie . . . I'm putting on my belt . . . I'm putting on my hat.

When our father gets to *Je mets mon chapeau*, Daddy is standing and has each one of us by the hand. Arlette and I know the wolf has nothing further to put on. He is ready to come and eat us and now we have to run. At this point our father swings us towards each other until Arlette and I collide. We mostly like it because we expect it.

Besides singing to us, he tells us nonsense rhymes we prattle back. Perhaps it is his way to keep us speaking French.

Maux de têtes	Headaches,
Têtes de veau,	Veal heads,
Vaudeville,	Vaudeville,
Ville de Pô,	The town of Pô,
Peau de balle,	Bullet sheath,
Balai de crin,	Straw broom,
Crin de cheval,	Horse hair,
Cheval de bois,	Wooden horse,
Bois de Campèche,	Wood from Campèche,
Pêche à la ligne,	Fish on the line,
Ligne de fond,	Plumb line,
Fonts baptismaux (da capo),	Baptismal fonts, (da capo)
Maux de têtes...	Headaches...

He has lots of friends and plays golf with Brazilian and American friends at the Itayangá Golf Club in Gávea, which is even further out of town than the American School in Leblon. When he and Arlette go for her golf lessons, they both wear matching brown and white shoes. Hers are called saddle shoes. His have nails called cleats at the bottom so he doesn't slip on the grass and he wears long white socks and knickers. Everyone says he is handsome. I like it that he always seems to be laughing, and finds something to make others laugh.

Daddy will play tennis, too, but he has to be dragged to the court. The ones who convince him to have a game are two Americans, Don and Laverne Murray. They are not as old as our parents or as their other friends. She wears her hair in coronet braids with gardenias woven in. She is very pretty, wears lipstick as bright as Esther Williams's and has a white, even smile. The older women gossip and say sailors chase after her, but my mother speaks up for her. "Don't be mean," she tells them.

"Come on, Benny," Mrs. Murray teases my father. "Come take us on."

My father smiles back, puts a cigarette in his white ivory holder, clamps down on it, and wedges it between his teeth. He takes his lighter from the right pocket of his long white tennis trousers, lights the cigarette with the familiar click, then exchanges the lighter for his highball on the table knowing we all are watching. In long white pants and tennis shoes, he walks slowly to the court, puts the highball down beside a bench, and positions himself on one side of the net while both Murrays go to the other. He always beats them, and they laugh through the hard-fought game. He then returns to the cool of the veranda of the Club, or goes inside for a game of cards or dice and orders a fresh highball.

"It's the cook's day off; I'm making crêpes," he announces one morning. Our kitchen is spacious, the ceilings are high. He puts on a béret. Mummy acts as sous-chef and prepares the batter, puts out the pan, the butter and, probably, lights the fire. A lighted cigarette dangles from the end of the *piteira*, and Daddy is humming. He pours the batter into the pan, swirls the batter in the melted butter, gets it just so, then says, "Now, I'm going to flip it." He sends the pancake sailing into the air so high it sticks to the ceiling. Arlette and I are in awe.

"Wait a bit. It will fall down, right back into the pan," he says with assurance, but it remains in place. We have no ladder tall enough for him to climb up to peel it off the ceiling, so he leaves it there, hands the pan to our mother, and the rest of the breakfast crêpes are hers, but we wish he had continued. We hear him going off to the dining room to do his crossword puzzles singing *Tout va très bien, Madame la Marquise*. The lovely silver-haired man who comes to polish our wood floors will be in the next day. Agenor thinks our father is funny and he won't mind scraping the pancake down somehow.

Sometimes our father takes us to a movie. When we go to watch the Looney Tune cartoons, Movietone news comes on first. It shows black and white pictures of soldiers in tanks or firing guns in places in a Europe we don't know. He does not speak about the soldiers, what side they are on, and I don't want to ask. Secretly, I know he does not like to see the news, nor to talk about it.

I know our father puts on the short-wave radio at home, but turns it off if Arlette and I walk into the living room. Through the crackle, I hear someone speaking in French. The only newspaper we see is *The Brooklyn Eagle* the Callahan sisters send us. They met our parents in Santiago, and moved to Rio at the same time they did, but when the National City Bank they worked for sent them back for good to Brooklyn, they kept in touch with us in every way they could. They send us *The Katzenjammer Kids* and *Little Lulu*, and roll up silk stockings for our mother inside the comic pages. They also send Didee Dolls, baby dolls with rubbery skin we feed tiny bottles of water to and who pee into diapers, dolls that make a mewing sound when tipped back and forth. These are treasures, all from the United States, the land of treasures, Hollywood musicals, bright red lipsticks and nail polish, spectator pumps, music of Carmen Miranda and Xavier Cougat, a Brazilian and a Cuban recognized even there. What world news is in *The Brooklyn Eagle*, we children don't see.

Our father's good humor turns only once that I can remember, and it is partially my fault. It is the day we wake up to heavy rain pelting against the shutters, the windows, running in the gutters, the air hot and clammy with humidity, a day not good for his lungs. It must be a Sunday because he is home.

Our mother, Arlette and I are restless. We do not want to read, play piano, do anything inside. The tempest is exciting and we want to be out in it. Mummy likes the rain; at least, she doesn't mind getting wet. She does not like the ocean, however. Not once in our years in Rio does she go into it. She is frightened of its undercurrents that take people out to sea, return them dead. It is our father who rollicks in the waves with us, teaches us to breathe the salt water into our noses and spit it out through our mouths so we won't get colds.

Our mother knows he likes the ocean. "Let's go walk on the beach. Come with us, Benny," Mummy asks. *Fous-moi le camp*, he dismisses us in rude French, laughing. He has the piteira in his mouth and is doing his beloved crossword puzzles. His ivory slide rule is at hand for when he finishes the puzzles. I love to watch him slide the rulers that fit into one another back and forth as he calculates numbers just for fun, or for some engineering plan he has in mind. I think he finds the numbers comforting. And then, there is his sketching pad by the slide ruler. These are his favorite pastimes, all close by.

If I pester him enough, he will make some straight-line drawings. His engineer's hand is sure, his perspectives just right.

For fun, he will sign a drawing with his signature flourish, a big B and huge tail of the J of Jean and the z in Benzacar. I try to copy his signature and the clarity of his letters. He is happy and settled for the day, and happy to tell us to go away.

"Come on, Benny!" our mother insists. Arlette and I do, too. He sees his three females needing to get out and comes with us.

We do not own slickers and the weather is hot, so whatever cover we throw on is not protective. Umbrellas are useless in the gale that blows in from the sea a block away from our home, the water salty on our faces, lips, tongues. Arlette and I open our arms to the storm and shriek back at it. We see Mummy's spirits lighten, her face full of smiles. By the end of three blocks, we are soaked, cooled off and satisfied, come home. Our father's three females are larking about, but he has gone quiet. He has taken a chill and we become terrified that he will get pneumonia again. We spend the rest of the day wrapping him in blankets, making him breathe over a steaming pot of water with camphorated Vicks Vaporub in it, hand him a whiskey. These seem to help as much as the sulfa drugs he has taken in the past. He does not get sick, but he is thickly silent. Arlette, Mummy and I will not be so careless of him again.

CHAPTER NINE

Grandparents

December, 1943

Querida familia,

We learn from our American friends at Esso that the Allies have, indeed, bombed the Ploesti gasoline storage tanks in a mission that sounded awful, and must have been since the reports of it all are unusually similar. They say the pilots had to fly low so as not to be detected by radar, but if they had to let the bombs go from so low down, how did the explosions not come up and destroy the following planes? Wonder how long it will be before Movietone news shows some footage? After the war?

I take comfort in my music. The trick is not so much to remember the Beethoven or Chopin, but to keep the piano from growing mold. Every conceivable form of life that needs heat and humidity thrives here. Our intestines supply what parasites love best. If we could hear the reproductive sounds of the millions of lower forms of life, they would over-ride the sounds of the war at its most explosive.

Abrazos, Queta

* * *

In Rio, among the ex-pats, grandparents are scant. The older generation has been left at home in any one of the numerous countries Nadia Ilyachenko, Helen Norman, the Hegel boys come from.

Brazilian families are full of token aunts and uncles, the tias and tios of every age who don't have to be related by blood to figure in the clan. Grown-ups all look old to us, so grandparents could be hiding in the crowd of families that gather at the Sunday lunches in Paisandú, or at the Chilean Embassy festivals we like for their music, dancing, and food, tastes we know from home.

Perhaps it is this apparent absence of grandparents that allows our parents to speak not at all of their own parents, and to relieve Arlette and me of much curiosity about an older generation, and why they might be absent from our lives.

Somehow, Arlette and I learn about Mummy's brothers and sisters. We know she has sisters in Santiago: Margot, Ines, and Rita. She didn't like Rita, though we never knew why. "We fought a lot," is all she says. How would it be not to like your sister? Arlette and I fight but it never occurs to me not to like her.

We know there are telegrams. We see them arrive, and we know they carry bad news. When our parents read one, they pass it back and forth silently between the two of them and look serious or scared. When I ask Mummy about her brothers, she says Edmond died in the First World War. "How do you know?" I ask her.

"They delivered a telegram," she says, but I don't know who "they" are, nor do I ask when she adds something I wish I had not heard. "It was the only time I saw my father cry." I don't know how to comfort this man who is grieving, who is related, who is unknown. There are too many unknowns and I feel guilty about the people, their feelings and mine.

"Where is your other brother?" I ask as if daring to scratch hives that already are bleeding but need to be gouged some more.

"Clément was killed in an explosion at a gasoline filling station in Mexico. There was a puddle of gasoline on the ground and a man carelessly threw a lighted cigarette into it."

Did a friend of the family see Clément catch fire, see him writhe until he died, or did he explode all at once? Had anyone tried to help? Had the friend come to Santiago to tell the family about it? How ever would you do that, I wonder; instead, I ask "How did you know?"

"We received a telegram," she answers, her quiet voice a mystery.

When our parents do not open telegrams in front of us, nor tell us what is in them, I am glad. I remind myself that I do not want to ask questions I might not like the answers to. I tuck these away and remain silent.

CHAPTER TEN

Diseases

le 4 février, 1944

Chère Margot,

We were at a gathering among Americans with the girls' godparents the other day and, on a social scale, Benny, the girls and I must seem a bit odd even here. I realized that on top of my Chilean-French status, and the girls being born in Brazil, the guardians we had chosen for them were a French couple for Denise, and a German and an American combination for Arlette. Fortunately, 'our' German had worked many years for the Otis Elevator in China and in different South American countries (in fact, might you have met him in Chile when Benny was there? Rudy Korsmeier, who has a great pugilist's nose and knuckles, jowls like the bloodhound our neighbors kept, and whose remedy for the confounding amoebas is lashings of castor oil!). He is a popular fellow here, like our German ophthalmologist, but I feel we all circle one another —or give the impression we are doing so—until we recognize where allegiances lie.

What actors we are on this impermanent stage! Changing languages helps as, chameleon-like, we also change stances and clothing appropriate to the occasion. Scene One: hat and gloves on independence day parties at different embassies; scene two: cocktail dresses for come-meet-the-new-chargé-d'affaires parties; scene three, tailored suits for office cocktail parties held in French, Italian, Hungarian, Russian,

American homes or at the Country Club. The women size up each other's looks and hairstyles, who speaks with whom, whose clothes are of freshest fashion, who the old-timers are from the more long-established companies, who really hobnobs with the artists. Of course, we all seek gossip, those sticky filaments of international spittle that fall from lips and become iridescent (oh, Margot, I hope you are laughing with me! This is not the life either one of us would desire!). How much tattle is useful when paired with information sifted from husbands and lovers remains mysterious; still, a faux pas here, another there and seed pearls of information emerge. Transfers of managers, access to supplies and travel show us the way the war is going.

The girls love it when they are invited to parties for grown-ups. The children know how to get along, share new dishes, and play hide and seek (once in a wine cellar hidden in a cave until they had to get the grown-ups involved in the search!). Denise has fallen in love with Planter's Peanuts our American neighbors across the street indulge her in.

The roles I play are socially invisible. I meet them in simple dresses for coping with daily life and accepting the unbridled generosity of our hosts. Only the Brazilians (which our girls pride themselves on being) are truly at home; the rest of us borrow and depend on the staggering beauty we live in, and on the lovely helpers we have who are soft, vulnerable, wish to comply and are desperate for kind direction. I think to myself I'd like direction, too, especially maneuvering round some of the superstitions that really interfere when the helpers let it. There are plenty of real diseases around without having to blame sorcerers. I pray I don't get sick.

Benny, along with his many working and golfing colleagues, makes his barriers liquid (you may take that in all ways). They dissolve. He hides from dissent and trouble more successfully than anyone I know, for which I'm grateful. I wonder sometimes, however, if the upper left tooth he has worn down from clamping hard on his cigarette holder isn't the result of his silenced but frayed nerves. He can worry but look dapper at the same time. Once transferred to his mouth, the holder rarely leaves.

Benny and I balance many imbalances with music—the classical radio programs for him, the piano for me, the popular radio programs and enjoyable carnival music, the dance class classics and Hollywood songs for the girls. And if all else is quiet, there is Nature that is chattering at us and begging for a listen. If this passes for a social life, it is not an intellectual one, but a mess of stuff that warrants a lot of musing! Et tu?

Je t'embrasse, Q.

* * *

"You have to stay out of the pools for a while." "Wash your hands and gargle." "You can't play with Jill because she's in quarantine," are things our mother tells us. We hear the grown-ups talking about dysentery, mumps, measles, diphtheria, whooping cough, polio and smallpox. They are very scared of these last two.

At school I have a friend, Ursula, who lurches around in heavy braces. She has come into my fifth grade class where most of us are ten years old, but she is at least twelve and looks developed like a grown-up lady. She had polio and had to miss school to learn how to walk again. The braces that hold up her body deform her school dress, box out her blouse, clatter and squeak where the leather straps and harness attach to the steel supports beneath her skirt and push down into her socks. We can see the metal bars go into her lace-up shoes.

A lot of kids shy away from her. She makes them feel uncomfortable and they don't know what to talk to her about. We all know it is impolite to stare at someone who looks different, but if I stand beside her, I can't stare; besides, I like to be with her. She is calm and quiet. The teachers let me be by her in the shade of the roof to watch the games that are going on in the schoolyard. If nothing else, we can listen to the shriek of the vultures, always near-by, or to the flag pole ropes hitting along the sides of the pole like the lanyards hitting the masts of sailing ships at anchor in the Bay.

Ursula asks me one day if my mother is Chilean and I learn that her family is part Chilean, part English. "I think I saw you at the Chilean Embassy the last time they had a party," she says. We talk about going to the Chilean Independence Day on the 18th of September at the Embassy, eating their *empanadas*, meat-filled pies, and *pastel de choclo*, a corn and onion and chopped meat kind of soufflé to which my mother also adds raisins. We both love the food and tell how we like to lose ourselves in the crowd so we can eat without having the grown-ups watch over us. The grown-ups dance the *cueca* waving white hankies over their heads and the air smells of *chiche* which Mummy tells me is a drink like cachaça. People get giddy on both. Ursula's English is soft, like my mother's, only Ursula never scolds.

When it comes time to go back to our classrooms, her face gets pink with the effort of walking. She shifts stiff-legged from her right side to her left and back again until she has managed to cover the short distance from the schoolyard to the classroom. Her face is sweaty and her blond curls stick to her cheeks by the time she gets there, but she never complains.

Our parents tell us Ursula is one of the lucky ones. We hear in whispers about relatives and friends of friends who die of polio or who live in an iron lung, a torpedo-like metal contraption into which patients must live because they cannot move their ribs in and out to breathe; the machine must do this for them. No one teases about people who have polio. Everyone is terrified of getting it.

Tante Chrisje, a good friend of our parent's bears smallpox scars on her face. She was born in Holland but traveled through Indonesia and China. I'm not sure where or when she caught the disease but, again, I hear our parents tell us she is one of the lucky ones. Not only did she have to stay quiet in a dark room for fourteen days, but she had high fevers and came out scarred. It is not nice to have pockmarks on your face, but it is better than dying.

We go for our smallpox vaccinations to one of the many communal health posts in the various districts of Rio. This one is on a back street of Copacabana. The people in charge are not full doctors. Most often, pharmacists are in charge; they deliver medicines without a doctor's prescription, and they give injections, a common form of giving medicine in Brazil.

Our smallpox vaccination is not by injection; it comes through a fountain pen, the kind that has a lever on the side that sucks up ink when someone pulls the lever up, shoots it out when the lever is pushed back down. The trick is to empty the chamber first, then lock it shut full of ink —or vaccine—when the lever is up. Children, grown-ups—patrons, gardeners, and maids alike — line up in a long queue along the sidewalk waiting to gain admission into the small room where the people in charge are preparing the pens.

We have a choice of being vaccinated on the back of the calf, the upper thigh, or the upper arm. We all will bear scars, so we are told to choose. I choose the back of my calf where it is impossible for me to see the procedure; I can worry about the scar later.

The vaccinator rubs the skin with alcohol, plunges the hand-cleaned pen nib into the vaccination vial, sucks up the liquid into the pen, then—with the nib—scratches the surface of our skin until the lines bleed. When there is fresh blood, he pulls the lever of the pen downwards so that the pen squirts the vaccine onto the bloody scratches. It hurts. We leave the wound open to the air until the vaccine has dried, then are given some gauze and adhesive tape to cover the sore spot. We must not scratch the wound or we are likely to spread the infection to other parts of our body where we also could develop scars. We wait for a scab to develop and, even then, we are not allowed to pick it off.

Infections are common. Keeping a wound wet and covered is enough to let an infection get started and, in Rio's hot humid climate, the bugs multiply as if they were in a fast-forward cartoon.

Our beloved dancing teacher, Dorothy Morgan Campos, who was a Rockette when she lived in New York, had a smallpox vaccination like the rest of us, only she develops the most florid infection Arlette and I have ever seen. Her thigh begins to turn red and the skin around the vaccination spot swells. By the time the pus rises in the center of the wound, it looks like a zinnia with its yellow dots in the middle, the pinks and purples and reds growing out from the center like an angry halo the size of a salad plate. It takes two weeks for the infection to dry, and months before Dorothy is free of scars and pain. No one teases about smallpox either.

And there are so many bugs.

"See the bumps on the zebus?" Mummy asks me when we are in the country one day. She is not referring to the big lump on the back that distinguishes these cattle from ordinary cows; she is pointing to the small bumps all over the animals. "Those are bugs that burrow their way into the animals' skins and make them very sick." We aren't supposed to touch the cows for fear of getting their diseases.

I think of the beach worm that gets under human skin. A friend of ours, David Ivy, had to have the doctor thread a crochet hook up the track the bug made under the skin of David's arm. When the doctor pulled out the worm, he said, "I hope I have it all." I know David did, too.

CHAPTER ELEVEN

The Spirits and the Popping Buttons

April, 1944

Queridos,

I am a month late in writing about the stunning facts you, too, have seen. Never did the American airmen (or anyone else, except maybe the animals) suspect the dramatic eruption of Mount Vesuvius in March — as if in exuberant recognition of the Allied Forces' arrival in Naples. Movietone news has been increasingly full of photographs of the current explosion and of the loss of aircraft in the Pompeiian airfield. Fortunately, it does not rival the destruction that buried Pompeii and Herculaneum centuries ago.

Whatever would you think or do when those first vomitings of destruction spewed up from the top of the volcano? (Chile has its share of live volcanoes, so we have an inkling!) The airmen knew enough to fly out of the pathway but had little idea of what would happen next. War and this, too?

The Disney cartoons follow, walloping the audience from one sort of fantastical experience to another, and life goes on.

Yours in dumbfound, Queta

* * *

"Queta, please," Mrs. L. calls in her loud voice that carries far from the phone receiver. "You have to come. Maria has locked herself in the dining room. She's convinced that someone's put a hex on her. She won't listen to the other maids and has started lighting candles in there. I'm afraid she's going to burn down the house. There's a crowd of servants, all as foolish as she is, that's come through our front gate and is gathering in our gardens. I don't know how they all know, but you'd think they've been drumming the tom-toms. I'm staying in our bedroom. Get your chauffeur to drive you over."

I remember every word because it is the kind of conversation I'm not supposed to overhear. I pretend to keep on reading the book that's in front of me, but next to Mrs. L.'s call, I lose interest in the Bobbsey twins.

Our chauffeur, João, is not ours. Like our father, he works for the Otis Elevator Company, and can drive our family only in emergencies. Our mother knows this, but she calls our father for permission to use João and the car. When our father hears it is Mrs. L. in trouble again, he sends him right over but is smart enough not to tell him why he is needed until he arrives at our house.

"João, we have to go help Mrs. L," are the only words João needs to begin sputtering reasons why he cannot stay with us. Mrs. L. has a personal chauffeur and word gets around in that group, as in all others. "Maria is in trouble. We have to help her." And to stop his complaining, she adds: "Denise is coming with us."

Why am I home and Arlette not? Have I pleaded a day home from school, or am I getting over another of the never-ending bouts of amoebas? Whatever the reason for my being with Mummy this day, I'm happy. I can ride in our wood-paneled station wagon seated with my mother in the back of the car, her hand in mine, and her fingers playing piano, as always. But music is not on the program. Mummy is distracted. "Stay by my side when we get out," she tells me with an urgency in her voice I like.

The L's house has a tall white-washed packed mud fence around it, and shards of sharp glass reflect colors on top of the wall. João draws up alongside the gate but will not continue into the drive or get out. With me hanging onto her skirt, my mother pushes through the crowd on the sidewalk and through the semi-opened gate. Guava, lemon and mango trees give shade within the garden and line the narrow snaky path to the front door.

Faz favor. Com licença, my mother softly asks permission to pass. She toes a line through the crowd of silent servants from other families until everyone hears Alice, another of Mrs. L's maids, whisper to them so the locked-in maid cannot hear: "It's Dona Queta and her daughter. Let them pass."

The people barely widen the graveled path to the steps leading up to the front door and we stumble through. The door opens at right angles to the steps so the people cannot look in. All they see is the three of us—Mummy, myself and the other maid—disappear into the dark wood hall within. Mrs. L. is nowhere in sight. I listen to the voices ping-pong from either side of the inner door.

Alice: "Maria, let me in please. Dona Queta is here."

Maria: "Don't let her in," growling and crying.

Alice: "She's not going to hurt you. You know her. She's brought Denise, the younger daughter, with her. They want to say hello."

Maria: "I'm not coming out and they are not coming in."

We smell the scent of burning candles seep under the door.

"You're going to make it too hot in there with all the candles."

"The bad spirit will come if it's dark."

"Open the windows then."

"NOOOOOOOO," Maria shrieks so loud I cover my ears and Mummy squeezes my hand so tight, it hurts. "He'll come through the open window, and then he'll take me to be his."

"Your friends are here, they will protect you."

"They are not my friends. One of them has set the spirit on me. I can't leave the house."

Mummy interrupts. "Maria. I have João here in the car. We have come to take you to safety, but you will have to come out of the room."

Maria keeps saying 'no' and Mummy keeps talking to her in a soft voice.

"Mrs. L. asked me to do this for you. She cares for you, Maria, or she would not have phoned. I brought Denise with me. She wants to see you. You can sing together—songs you both know: *Eu sou o pirata da perna de pao*—you remember the pirate song, the pirate who has a wooden leg? You will have each one of us on either side of you. No one would think of harming us, and they won't harm you while you are with us."

I think of our parents saying to us: "If you don't believe in Macumba, it won't hurt you." I don't. It strikes me as too much trouble.

Mummy and I wait at the L's house until thirst or hunger or tiredness frees Maria from panic. I am sitting on the floor by then and do not pay attention to much besides the sound of the door latches unlocking. When Maria comes out, she is all hot and sweaty and trembling and I take her by the hand. The crowd starts muttering when they see us, but they don't move in on her or on us. Our small-framed mother pushes me, then Maria, and then squeezes herself into the back seat of the car. Maria cannot turn around or back up.

João stays in the driver's seat and will not help. I'm not sure if he is afraid of Maria or if he is afraid some of his friends in the yard might think he's taking sides on behalf of Mrs. L.

Mummy gives directions to Posto Seis, one of the many emergency huts along the beaches. She perches on one hip as we shoot off. When we enter a tunnel, Maria howls the length of it and I hear popping noises. When we get to the end of it, I realized the popping sounds came from Maria's tearing at my mother's dress. Where buttons had been, there are now shredded scars.

Doctor's assistants run the emergency huts. They store bandages and splints for putting broken bones together, ointments for sunburns—or burns at home—eye and ear drops.

A senhora precisa um calmante, they say, understanding Maria needs a medicine to calm her. They give her an injection and Maria goes sort of floppy.

"New fears will follow," Mummy says under her breath as we leave Maria with the men to watch over her until Mr. L. picks her up. Then Mummy collects all the buttons she can find from the floor of the station wagon.

PART TWO

A Wartime Vacation

December, 1944 –
February, 1945

CHAPTER TWELVE

A Wartime Vacation

September, 1944

Queridos,

Chile has publicly joined the Allies in philosophy, if not in sending troops. Welcome!

We are glad to know you are well, not suffering any more shortages than the rest of us. Those who have cars here are having to convert to the coal-burning 'gasogenios'—dangerous and hot. A young American couple we know were driving to Petropolis in one of them last week. The wife, a beautiful woman (looks like Joan Fontaine in the movies) called Laverne Murray, was sitting in the back seat with their young son. The husband, Don, was driving. "Don," she said, "it's so hot back here, I feel I am burning up." "You're always exaggerating, Laverne. We're nearly there." And that's when he saw flames leaping out of the coal canisters attached to the back of their car. They got out alive, but the car was incinerated.

Actually, the poor Murrays recently were run out of their quartz business by his partner, so Benny is helping them get back to the States to get enough capital to start again. Don's wonderfully productive island in the mouth of the Amazon River is his no longer, nor are any of the contracts he drew up. He probably will be able to reclaim most of his losses, but not in time to support him and his family. Have no idea how the partner got away with this, except through the time-honored tradition of bribes, but the reality is the Murrays need help now. Nice to be able to give it.

I must run. I will pretend that, like St. Exupéry, I'm on the mail plane over the Andes coming to give you hugs, Queta.

* * *

Arlette and I have a friend called Sally. Actually, she is Arlette's friend because Arlette is two and a half years older than I am, and Sally is one and a half years older than Arlette. They put up with me when they have to because our mothers are friends. Sally has two shoulder-length blond braids, very light blue eyes, and wears lace-up Indian Walk shoes from the United States where her parents come from. Arlette and I call Sally's mother "Tia Mildred" the way we make most of our parent's friends into aunts and uncles. Sally's father, Clarence Wiseley works for the National City Bank and everyone calls him "Wise" but we call him Mr. Wiseley. The Wiseleys have invited our mother and us to spend the summer in Jundiaí with them.

Our mother, Arlette and I are at the Wiseley's airy house on the ocean avenue in Ipanema when Tia Mildred tells us about the plan. With her bony fingers, she is arranging fragrant lilies and grasses in tall vases she then places on the living room floor so that the maids can fill them with water and leave them there.

"The flowers are a distraction; this way, you don't need furniture," she tells Mummy.

I glance around and notice there are not even enough chairs for people to sit in if they wanted to listen to someone play the white piano, the only big piece of furniture in the room. I think of our own house with its dark jacaranda dining room table, six chairs and heavy buffet, and of the dark comfy couch and upright piano in our living room. Not much furniture there, either, but at least we can sit, listen to the radio, or to Mummy playing the piano.

"Don't you want to go out to play?" Tia Mildred asks me.

The last time Arlette and Sally let me play with them, I had to wait for two hours outside the garden gate watching lizards and butterflies and patting the dog while they went inside to plant rice paddies by themselves. I don't want to play like that again, so when Arlette and Sally go off immediately upon our arrival today, I shake my head no and push into my mother's side with a force she understands will keep me there during our visit.

Why would I go to play alone when I know the maid will be bringing in tea and cake and pieces of pineapple, guavas and papaya to eat? Arlette and Sally will be eating these in the kitchen, plus lots of coconut sweets the cook will stuff them with. They must have special sugar rations, I think, and wonder who goes to stand in line from the Wiseley household. I stop day-dreaming and start listening to the grown-ups, something I like.

"The Gordinhos have lent us their farm for the entire summer," Tia Mildred says.

"Gordinho" means a little fat person, so I like the family right away and listen carefully to her description of their coffee plantation on a high plateau of red earth.

"Jundiaí is northwest of São Paulo, high in the mountains, so it will be cool there, better than the heat and humidity here in Rio. They are letting us have it a second year in a row as a thank you to Wise for giving the Gordinhos a bank loan.

'We need to build an office in the center of downtown São Paulo and want to see it finished in eighteen months,' the Gordinhos told him.

"Of course, Wise never protected himself by reminding them the war was on, and like everything else—sugar, flour, butter—construction material had to be brought in by road or sea."

I get the impression she is telling her story to teach me and not for my mother's benefit.

Tia Mildred's hands busy themselves placing pots of gardenias brought in from the garden, and calls the maid to bring in tea. (I certainly am not about to move.) "Wise knew that land travel meant trucks, which meant gasoline, which was out of the question. Trains had slowed down because of a lack of coal, and sea travel meant ships risked being torpedoed by the Germans. All three forms of travel guaranteed delay. The fastest any building had been constructed in São Paulo had been six years, and that was before the war.

"But Wise liked these people. They were hard-workers like himself, so he decided he would become the contractor as well as the banker. Wise kept track of every gasoline shipment, made sure the shipments were sent to the right people, made sure the right people filled the right gas tanks."

Tia Mildred continues with all the details and thoughtfully keeps me quiet by filling my plate with tart guava paste and quiejo de Minas, a bland rubbery cheese.

"He oversaw each delivery of sand, cement, steel, wood, and nails. He drew up blueprints to show where each file, desk, telephone bank would go in the new building and, over a four-day holiday week-end before the Gordinhos were supposed to move in, he accompanied the movers to assure himself that every desk, every chair, every phone was set in place and functioning. He made the eighteen-month deadline."

I like hearing the part about the phones. We are not permitted to use ours at home and know phones are very special, for emergencies only, though Mummy sometimes speaks on it to her friends. I picture the phones Mr. Wiseley has to set in place the way I have seen in American movies with a lady sitting in front of a board full of holes that she pokes a plug with bouncy wires into, and then the light over the plug goes out until the call is finished.

"The Gordinhos were properly impressed and grateful. They offered us their summer home, the farm in Jundiaí."

I stuff myself full of the fragrant sweets that Tia Mildred keeps handing me from the tea tray, drink a hot milky cup of tea, and hear her tell Mummy that she and Sally had gone alone last summer and spent endless days in endless rain. Sally's only companion, Pinote, the farm hand, took her riding with him for hours at a time while he finished his chores, an arrangement they both liked. Tia Mildred's main companion, however, was the cook and there was only so much they could organize and talk about.

Mr. Wiseley, like our father and other men who work for American companies in South America, doesn't seem to take vacations. It had been a lonely summer for her. Wouldn't we like to come with them this year? Sally is eleven, Arlette nine, and I am six and a half and I have heard the whole invitation. My mother doesn't speak, but I will hear her repeat the story of Mr. Wiseley for our father, and I know Daddy will say yes.

In early January, in the heat of summer, we five take the train which follows a path south between the Atlantic Ocean and the mountainous Serra do Mar from Rio to São Paulo. We change trains at São Paulo for the spur that will climb the hills inland and get off at a one-room station with a wooden table that serves as an occasional ticket office. In Jundiaí, the Gordinhos have arranged for a chauffeur to meet us and our luggage, and we drive the last miles to the farm in a station wagon.

The road is bumpy, climbs and turns, and I feel carsick. Although the drive cannot take more than three quarters of an hour, the chauffeur lets us out for two runs. We gulp in the crisp air fussed at by the winds of the plateau. The air smells of the sweet pungent grass called capim, a scent I want to fill my lungs with forever and rub into my skin. On one of these runs, Sally opens her arms to the moving air and her mouth to laughter until a bee flies into it and stings her. She stops short in a confusion of pain and outrage. After her first tears, Sally tells and re-tells how the bee stung the inside of her mouth until she is tired and the ache is gone.

The car climbs the hills to the farm under blue skies and cumulus heaps, curves round the stables, and pulls up by the yellow mimosas and blue jacarandas that cover the front of the porch where we will sit for hours that summer.

It is here our mothers will knit and talk, plan menus for the cook, decide which questions on farm management they can answer, which should be directed to the Gordinhos back in São Paulo. It seems it is Tia Mildred who does all the deciding. Our mother is new to this place, to the owners, and is happy to entrust the running of the days to Tia Mildred.

CHAPTER THIRTEEN

Jundiaí – Pinote

This is letter #1, January, 1945

¡Holá! mi familia,

Here we are on an abandoned coffee plantation in the hills outside of São Paulo, courtesy of one of Benny's American colleagues who works for National City Bank, my old stamping grounds in Santiago. (Too bad they don't need a secretary anymore!) His wife, Mildred, is a friend of mine through the American School the children attend.

It is a long story on how we are here, but the reality is we are out of Rio's heat for two months and have somewhere other than Pouços de Caldo or Friburgo or Tijuca to go to for a scant week or two. The girls have Mildred's daughter, Sally, to play with. She is almost two years older than Arlette, and they are good friends. Benny and Mildred's husband will be bachelors (or so we suppose) for the summer as the war keeps them at their desks more so than usual.

As to the war, I want to hear the news; I don't want to hear the news. Our isolation quashes rumor for a bit. I will allow nature to distract me, and there is an abundance of her glories here. The wind slaps the palm trees and whips up the scents of capim, that tough-leaved grass, and of the warm red earth. We wake to the perfume of things vegetative and of insects that have a scent of their own.

I look forward to riding the surprisingly nice horses they have here, and to a reprieve from the Country Club and any social activities. I've brought some Dumas—*père et fils*—in case the girls want some stories, and a bunch of Colette's works, nothing heavy. I shall miss my piano.

We have a cook and a *fazendero*, a farmhand, named Pinote. These two will do nicely. Mildred and I are practiced housewives and we'll work out the division of labor. I imagine meals will be simple. Rice and beans seem to be in good supply, and collards grow like weeds. We can get corn from the farm, so I will work on a *pastel de choclo*. The chickens running around will give us good *cãnjas*, soups into which we add all the greens we can find, plus rice. The chickens themselves are too tough to eat except by boiling for hours. The girls eat indiscriminately, so we can invent to our hearts' content. There are bananas, mangoes, guavas, coconuts and sugar cane galore for them to fill up on.

With gasoline at such a premium, we have no car. The *fazendero* can ride the horse into town, but it is not an efficient way to bring home perishables; besides, we'd rather have him on the property in case who-knows-what pops up. We have a phone for emergencies, but no radio. It will be both a relief not to hear the war news, and a worry wondering what's going on. Benny will be able to keep on the short wave without fear of interruption by the girls; otherwise, I imagine he will be going on his rounds of golf and bouts of tennis. Heavens knows how I get the mail out to you, but we'll figure out a way. I am numbering my letters as I'm sure they'll go out in a bunch.

Abrazos, Queta

*　*　*

"Pinote will look after the children," Tia Mildred announces as she waves in the slight Indian man who stands at the threshold of the kitchen. He has taken off his *tamancos* so the thick wooden soles won't soil the floor or clatter too much. Here in Jundiaí, the earth is so soft that it absorbs the sounds of the flapping shoes. He keeps still, straw hat in hand. Sally rushes up to him and gives him a hug. They are almost the same size. He doesn't put his arms around her, but smiles with such pleasure, we know he is happy to see her again.

"I can help you round up the cattle," she tells him.

"Leave the poor man alone, Sally. We'll see how things develop," Tia Mildred interrupts. She is trying to protect Pinote from having too much to do, but she has hurt her daughter's feelings. Sally stands back while Tia Mildred introduces Pinote to our mother, Dona Queta, Arlette and me. He bows to my mother, darts his green eyes at Arlette and me as if to say "We will get to know each other well and soon." He tells us his only sow, Esmeralda, has had a litter of thirteen piglets.

"If anyone gets near her babies, she will attack you. She weighs more than I do," he says, his right hand gesturing over his head as if the sow is taller, too. He warns our mothers to not let us get near her.

We want to see the piglets, so Sally takes charge.

"Let's go see Esmeralda tomorrow," she says one evening soon after our arrival. "We'll go before dawn so no one sees us."

She, Arlette and I, who share a room, escape unnoticed into the still black morning and keep to the huge bushes. Pinote, ever wakeful and mistrustful, knows he is responsible for us on the property and does not welcome a twenty-four hour guessing game. He hears us coming, notices our three figures moving among the bushes. He notes another movement in the bushes, knows not to yell as the black-spotted cat is keeping its distance, but Pinote's heart is in his mouth; after all, he is responsible for these three disobedient girls, and the jaguar's ability to attack on moment's notice is notorious. His fangs and claws would be on one of us before we heard him pounce, but the cat must not be hungry. We arrive innocent and unharmed.

Light breaks with the sudden tropical dawn by the time we cozy up to the fence and, with our own squeals, we count the piglets. Despite her enormous size, Esmeralda has lightning trotters and gives us chase from the fence that separates her from us. We retract in terror from the fence, but glue ourselves back to it the moment she returns to her brood.

Que boa sorte! What good luck, our ally Pinote later says to our mothers. They think he refers to Esmeralda's not ripping into us.

Pinote's voice begins to follow us, whether he is there or not.

"*Cuidado.* Be careful. Be careful of snakes, of spiders," he calls after us. Like a guardian spirit, he materializes on the porch. He has come barefoot from the kitchen through the shadowed house to consult with our mothers about his last-minute tasks for the day, to report on ailing children and animals, to ask advice. He addresses our mothers, but it is to Sally, Arlette and to me that he is speaking. "The tarantulas hide in banana leaves and they can jump, you know."

No banana leaves here, so no need to worry we decide, and we're off to zig-zag in and out of the shushing rows of corn and sugar cane whose stalks are higher than we are and where tarantulas also like to hide. We gather corn cobs and take them to our mothers who show us how to make corn husk dolls. Over the summer, we make dozens, give the dolls different corn silk hair styles, dress them up in scraps of colored cloth from our mothers' sewing baskets, name them, leave them behind.

Occasionally, our mother, Arlette and I separate from Sally and Tia Mildred. Mummy loves to ride. She used to ride a lot in Chile because her family kept horses. We have seen photographs of her riding them. There are enough horses at the farm for everyone, but we like two in particular: *Relámpago* and *Trovão*, Lightning and Thunder. One is brown and the other is black, and Pinote tells us one is fifteen hands high, the other seventeen. I don't know how to measure this, but both animals look huge. Mummy helps us mount the horses by cupping her hands so we can step into them while she pushes us up into the saddles.

We know Sally rides with Pinote to round up the cattle, but Arlette and I get to ride with our mother. She takes us separately so she can concentrate on how well we handle the horses. We follow hilly paths through trees that give welcomed shade, and laugh at the loud chorus of macaws, frogs, geckos and crickets. We break into fields yellow with grain and sunshine and still full of insect sounds.

"Do you know horses love to swim?" she asks one day. I follow her on my own horse into a wide pond where I learn that horses swim as quietly as they drink. I sit splashless on the bare back of this sweet-smelling animal. "It is better for the horse if you hang on tight to his mane and slip off his back until you are swimming side by side, but don't let go of his mane!" Mummy tells me. Then comes the thrill of clambering back on as the horse starts his awkward bolt up the pond bank and the world becomes noisy again with the horse's snorting, the jangle of his bridle, and the chunk of his shoes on stones.

It is hard not to sing through the sun-burning and water-cooling days riding with my mother. She sings, too.

While out on the horses, we stop along the way to collect tiny green frogs to put in match boxes Mummy thinks to bring. The frogs seem tame, don't hop away, but tuck themselves into the boxes as if they like it in the small dark spaces that smell of balsa wood and sulphur. We take them to show Tia Mildred who never wanders far from the farmhouse. After she has harrumphed something about them without curiosity, we let the frogs go free near some water.

CHAPTER FOURTEEN

Jundiaí –
The Coffee Pool

Letter #2, January, 1945

Queridos,

Finding a physical place to read and write is the big challenge here. The porch is perfect, but Mildred likes it, too. She is a talker. As you remember, I am not; on the other hand, she did not have my benefit of learning how to steal time with babbling siblings around. No wonder she was lonely last summer with no one to talk to except the farmer. Like cats, we are marking our boundaries.

It is amazingly cool and dry here as we are at 760 meters. The skies command attention with clouds so dramatic, it's as if a celestial painter plays with different palettes every twenty minutes. Watching the storms come up is exciting and terrifying. They are presaged by sudden winds and an equally sudden drop in temperature so that by the time the rains fall—and it can be a matter of seconds—it is decidedly cool. Thunder and lightning accompany almost all rain storms. The sound of the water falling on the huge leaves of the banana trees and philodendra are the best music on the farm; in fact, other than the racket of insects, parrots and squealing pigs, it's pretty much the only music. I miss the staff in Rio for their constant singing and whistling of the carnival songs, or even of an advertising ditty on the radio that sticks in your ears too long.

We have few mosquitoes and flies thanks, no doubt, to the bats and thousands of spiders lurking about. I fear the spiders. About one month before we left Rio, one bit Denise on the calf. She ended up with such a severe reaction, that she had to stay in bed for three days in a darkened room, and was delirious with fever, so we do what we can to make sure spiders are not in our shoes and clothes in the morning, or waiting for us in our pajamas at night. The mosquito nets we keep around the beds at all hours seem to be of limited help.

Otherwise, I long to get out on the horses and to take the girls with me, one at a time. Mildred does not ride, so she is reluctant to let me go. These are niggling complaints compared to what's happening in the war world. Many soldiers would exchange a bed of spiders for what they are enduring. I need your news.

Con el amor de siempre, Queta

* * *

It is raining so hard that the only way we can breathe through the water is to lower our heads so that the space between our noses and mouths keep dry. We could use our hands to cup an air space the way we do when we go under the waterfall with the horses, but our hands are fists full of mud. Arlette, Sally and I are skidding in our bare feet, shrieking, falling down and laughing in the big shallow rectangles the farmer uses to dry coffee beans. Seconds ago, the mud was dry dirt, but the sudden storm has added water and beaten the dry ingredients as if this pool were a mixing bowl in the kitchen. The water is already up to our ankles, but it is not too cold and there is no thunder or lightning.

The reason they are not drying coffee beans is because of the war, our mothers tell us. It's why we can play here. The Gordinhos are not growing coffee anymore. All the young men have gone into the army, so there is no more help. Also, there is no gasoline, so the Gordinhos can't send the coffee beans to market. Because there is no gasoline, trucks and cars have to carry on their backs tall round tanks that are filled with coal. They smell terrible. Lots of cars catch fire, like the one our friends the Murrays were in.

We hardly go in cars in any case and, right now, we are running in circles in the pools. We scream and run and fall and run some more until one of us hears Mummy calling through the loud rain. We run to hide in the near-by barn.

"Shhh!" Sally, the first to recover her breath, giggles and pants at us. "She doesn't see us. Don't let her know we are here."

Arlette and I would follow any of Sally's order. Not only is she older than we are, but she speaks much better English than I do. In Rio, Arlette and Sally don't let me join their games. They pretend they do important projects like plant a rice paddy, and I pretend to believe them.

"Don't you think Mummy will be worried?" I ask when I hear her repeated calls for us. She is carrying raincoats for the three of us and the silliness of that makes us laugh so hard, we nearly cry.

"We better tell her," says Arlette. We see Mummy stop and watch the rain pour off her head and shoulders. Her flowered dress is glued to her body, her hair has come undone from the roll she wears around her head and it is getting in her eyes. She can't push it away because her arms and hands are full of our raincoats. She stops as if listening carefully, then turns to walk back to the house in the rain that is bucketing over her while we are drying out in the heat and shelter of the hay-smelling barn.

The barn has two stories. We have scrambled up a ramp to the top one where the young goat, *Manè*, is tied by a rope to one of the poles. His little horns are trying to break through the skin and they must hurt or itch because he keeps grinding his head into us.

"It must feel like a tooth ache," Sally says as we all try to get him to butt against us. "See his eyes and the slits in them? The holes in our eyes are round," she says with authority. Of course, she is right. Sally is always right until the day she joins Pinote to round up the cattle. She did this with him all last summer, when she and her mother were at the farm, so Sally really knows how. She is not gone long before she is back with Pinote and the white zebus, the cows with the humps behind their heads. She doesn't have to brag. She knows we are impressed especially because Pinote has never asked us to round up the cattle with him. She is the only one with those privileges. She hops off the back of the horse and we notice she has on shorts. "Sally," I say to her, "you told us never, never go on horseback with shorts on because the saddle can pinch your skin and because you can get ticks."

"This was an emergency," she says. "Pinote needed me."

I believe her grudgingly. I see no marks on her legs. Bug bites can make terrible sores. I have seen them on the animals' hides, so why not on ours?

The rain stops as suddenly as it came.

When we get back to the farm, our mysterious mothers say nothing, not "Where have you been?" or "We were worried about you," or "Haven't you any sense in your heads among the three of you?" They run baths for us, give us clean clothes, and take away the dirty ones.

CHAPTER FIFTEEN

Jundiaí – Illness

Letter #3, February, 1945

Margot, chérie,

The farm hand rode in from the train station with a packet of letters from all of you this afternoon. You can't imagine my joy! It was reassuring to read you've had no big earthquakes even though there are the usual familiar tremors, such as Rita still fighting, but less since I, her nemesis, left home. Once the baby of the family, I had the nerve to show up after her. Not much I could do about it. I can imagine why you'd like to leave familial arguments.

Thank you for your snippets of war news. The bombings and starvation and deprivations are all unimaginable or, perhaps, too imaginable and therefore odious. I feel it is not so long ago we lost Edmond to the First World War, and Clément to another kind of explosion. Two brothers gone up in flames. How have Maman and Père stood it? I'm sure the war contributes to my sense of transience in this world. I don't want to be gloomy, but am today. Maybe it's the reminder of the war that obliterates civilian and military life at random, or maybe it is all the diseases here on the farm and in the cities.

The girls have to be guarded against all sorts of bug, spider and snake bites. (Denise shows no caution in anything and, therefore, gets bitten.) Besides polio, there is constant amoebic dysentery. I worry about Benny's lungs—a mess—but he covers up his coughs that make him turn purple *as if his gasping for breath is a bagatelle. Can he possibly be aware how many minutes the girls and I have reflexively held our own breaths with him until his oxygen-starved body finally takes in the air he needs so much (and ours do, too). My bout with dyphtheria at Oberlin branded itself in memory. I do not want anyone to go through that. The farmhand himself was coughing like crazy when he returned with the letters. Uncharacteristically, he rode his horse all the way to the porch instead of leaving it in the barn. We said nothing, but worried when we heard his labored breathing. Of course, he would not complain.*

A bientôt, chérie. Je t'embrasse. Queta

P.S. Is it true that St. Ex disappeared in the Mediterranean? Is it possible not to find him? If you hear anything that sounds like something more stable than rumor, please let me know. Did he write 'Le Petit Prince' as some sort of preview of his own death? A sad loss, if true.

* * *

"Pinote has pneumonia," I hear my mother tell Tia Mildred.

Dona Ana, Pinote's wife, had run to the farmhouse that morning to say Pinote was sick. Our mother left the breakfast table to follow Dona Ana to the cabin and returned with the news.

"Arlette, you and Sally stay here with the cook. Denise, come with us," Mummy says.

"Why aren't Arlette and Sally coming?" is my first question. Arlette, Sally and I have done everything together this summer. Maybe they don't like me any more and want to be free of me, I think, but then Tia Mildred interrupts my chance to feel sorry for myself with a sharp "SHUSH" and "You're going to help us carry things to the cabin. Hold out your arms," She piles the cleaned and folded flannel cloths onto my outstretched arms. I look to my mother for comfort or explanation, but there is none. She stares unblinking like a lizard at me, and keeps me silent. Her stare is not friendly and I am hurt and fearful at the same time that I am excited to be the only one to be included in something she considers far more important than my feelings.

At the cabin, Mummy bends over Pinote, touches his forehead and listens to his breathing. She begins to fan him as if her hand can get rid of his temperature, but it only makes the flies go away. The wide mud walls of Pinote's two-room cabin keep out the heat, but the air doesn't move in and out of the tiny windows very well. Pinote lives here with his wife and their three children. They have had a child once a year and this year's baby looks like the runt in Esmeralda's litter except Esmeralda had the thirteen babies all at once. They squeal outside the cabin.

I know the word pneumonia because my father has had it three times. The last time, a few months ago, a friend called Mummy from the office and said: "Benny's sick and you'd better pick him up when the car arrives; he can hardly walk." Daddy knew we would be watching for him from the front balcony. He must have forced the driver to stop in the middle of the street to show us how strong he was. The driver, João, loves him, would do what my father asks, and calls him "Doutor, " a mark of respect, even though my father isn't a doctor.

We watched my father get out on the traffic side—there was no traffic in those war years—then collapse like a ballet dancer whose legs had turned to honey. He caught himself on the side of the car and, by that time, my mother, Raimunda and João were down at his side half carrying him upstairs.

The remedy for pneumonia is to put hot mustard cataplasms on peoples' backs. The poultices are so hot they sometimes leave burns and blisters on the skin. Our father hates them but he was too sick and weak to quarrel. He grunted and panted with a gravelly noise like waves going back and forth over small stones on the shore. This time, the American doctor they called came with something special.

"They are using this on the soldiers in Europe now. It's very good at killing the kind of germs you have, but it's made with horse serum and you may have a bad local reaction to it. I don't think you have a choice, Benny. This time is worse than before."

How bad exactly was before, I wondered. I was standing on bare feet on the cool tile floor outside their shuttered bedroom. It was exciting because everyone was so serious. What was a bad local reaction? Of course Daddy wasn't going to die. He hadn't before and he wouldn't now.

"His temperature is 104 degrees," the doctor announced in a voice that sounded angry. He tucked the thermometer into its case as if he had read my mind that I might want it. I wanted to break the thermometer and empty the mercury inside it onto my palm the way the dentist put pellets of mercury into my hand to play with if I had been obedient. Today, though, I knew was different. I tried to keep out of the way of the grown-ups, and even of Arlette.

I saw the doctor take out a syringe, a little bottle with some thick yellowish liquid in it, then put the needle in the bottle to pull up the liquid. He held the needle up to the light, and tapped the syringe. I kept my eyes on it. I was always getting injections for one thing or another and hated them, hated the pharmacist who came to give them, hid behind the pot in the bathroom until they pulled me out shrieking. How could I help my father not get it, but just as I was watching, the doctor put the needle into Daddy's bottom. He groaned.

The next day, my father's temperature was almost normal, he was breathing more easily, and he laughed as if he were the most surprised of all until he tried to turn onto the cheek the doctor had given him the injection in. "Come see," he said to us all. There was a bump on his bottom the size of the ostrich egg we had seen in a zoo. "It hurts more than my breathing," he said, but he had been cured by what the doctor called a "miracle drug," and in six weeks, the bump and bruising were gone. Arlette and I insisted on seeing how it got smaller day by day until there was only yellow where the egg had been.

"You are the first civilian I've tried penicillin on, Benny. We both were lucky. For heaven's sake, stop smoking."

Now, though, I am in Pinote's house. I feel his fever is drying out the water that has spilled on the packed mud floor. We have no penicillin. We don't even have a nearby doctor. I feel terrible about the mischief we've caused him. I hold the bowl and the mustard powder and the cloths Mummy and Tia Mildred will need. Dona Ana—Mrs. Pinote—boils water on the wood fire she prepares their rice and beans on and keeps the children away.

"Hand me the bowl, Denise," my mother says. "When I have put the mustard in, ask Dona Ana to bring me the boiling water. Ask her nicely, then stand out of her way."

I do as told, watch Tia Mildred mix the water and mustard with a long wooden spoon, and put in one of the flannel cloths while my mother is lifting up Pinote's shoulders and slipping the nightshirt off his skinny body. His ribs stick out in his Indian tan skin and his rattling breaths sound the way my father's did. The cloth is so hot, Tia Mildred lifts it out with a spoon so it will drip over the bowl, and when she and my mother think the compress won't burn their fingers or his back, they take the wet cloth and plop it onto his back, pulling it out at the corners with their fingertips. "*E quente*, It's hot!" he rasps with barely enough energy to weep.

CHAPTER SIXTEEN

Jundiaí – Pushing Limits

If there is a radio in the house, I don't hear it. We don't get newspapers. There is a black phone on the wall, but I see Tia Mildred speaking into the receiver only once, and I don't know what the call is about. We give no thought to what our fathers are doing, nor to what is happening in the larger world. Our interests are much more immediate and center on Jundiaí.

Ever since the three of us got away to see the piglets, we have not been allowed to share a room together; instead, Arlette and I sleep with our mother in one room, Sally sleeps with hers in another.

"Wait, let me see." Mummy does not let us get out of bed until she has come to judge if it is all right to simply shake off the *bichos*—a word for bugs of all sorts—from the netting that drapes over our beds overnight, like tents. Sometimes, she thinks there is one bug over another that needs killing before falling on us. There is a broom in a corner she keeps for this purpose.

Mummy makes wonderful faces. She can look Chinese or imitate a monkey, but the face she makes every morning while she clears the nets is one of fear. This is not a job she enjoys and we become squeamish seeing her discomfort.

One morning Mummy tries to brush what she thinks is a tarantula from the net and across to our bedroom threshold, but when she raises the broom to give the spider its final push outside, the tarantula is nowhere to be seen.

"Look out," Arlette and I shout together. We see the spider ready to spring at Mummy from the side bristles of the broom. Mummy shrieks, lashes at the spider, beats and beats it until it is dead.

"Next time, throw away the broom," Pinote tells her when he is up and around again and hears the story. "That spider is called a Brazilian Meandering Spider. It is more poisonous than a tarantula, but you don't want a bite from either."

Pinote had tried to protect us from the *bichos* when he was well. He got a can of FLIT, a spray to kill the insects. It smells oily and we don't like to breathe it in, so he breathed it for us, sprayed our bedrooms while we were having dinner. It was supposed to keep the bugs from collecting on the nets in the morning, but they were always there. Our mothers will not let Pinote spray the FLIT again. "Not with those lungs."

While Pinote gets better, Mummy and Tia Mildred keep us closer to the house, which Arlette, Sally and I dare each other to explore. I love and fear this house. "Slaves built it in the eighteen hundreds," Tia Mildred tells us. "Look, the walls are three feet thick." Its walls inside and out are whitewashed, and the windows have shutters that close like doors and are too far from me to reach from inside. In the hurting light of summer, the enormous shaded rooms are dark and cool with their carpet-less expanses of polished worn wood or stone floors.

"See if you can find the secret bathroom; I found it last year," Sally challenges one morning. We are in the dark wood-paneled dining room. Sally gives a big hint by starting to sidestep with her back to the wall. She stops at the kitchen door. "Go on," she says. "Start on the other side of this door and keep going," so we do until a panel gives way and we fall backwards into a spider-filled room. I have learned nothing from Mummy's morning toils. *Bichos* line the bathtub, the toilet, the sink. The first few times, I never try falling into the bathroom unless Arlette or Sally comes in with me, or is within shouting distance. Suppose I got stuck? There is something contrary about the inner latch. Suppose it didn't work? I fall into the room to cure my fear for the first time, and the next, and the next, but fly out of there with no cure and no delay. There is something contrary about me, too, as I measure my boundaries of fear and try to stretch them. Arlette and Sally do not continue with this folly and, eventually, I, too, stop.

The farmhouse is one story high, but there is a large cellar with broad, shallow marble steps leading down. Sally, Arlette and I memorize every inch of the underground mud walls, skirt the massive pool table we are not allowed to touch, peer with relief at the white light coming from above our head—and beyond our reach—through semi-circular windows up at ground level. We dare each other to go into a dark moldy room where the wine is kept.

"It's like the oubliette," Arlette tells me

"What's that?" I ask.

"It's a hole in the ground people put children in that they don't like. Then they put a lid on top and forget about them."

"Forever?" I ask in terror, recalling the secret bathroom.

"Maybe," Arlette answers, but the idea of being forgotten in a black hole is enough to keep us outside peeking into the wine cellar from the door and not crossing the threshold. After all, Tia Mildred drinks Bourbon, and Mummy doesn't seem to drink anything at all. Who would come to look for us?

When we have scared ourselves enough, we run up the easy stairs out through the veranda and past our mothers faster than a call can stop us.

"*Vamos ir là!* Let's go there!" Sally points. Her finger directs us into unspecified openness of greenery and blue sky that shrieks at us: "Run to me!" And we do.

CHAPTER SEVENTEEN

Jundiaí – Stories

Letter #4, February, 1945

Querida Susana,

You have been such a faithful correspondent, an informative and fun niece. I love your flights of curiosity. Did you know they called me "Batty" at Oberlin? I guess they thought I was pretty nuts. Maybe you take after me.

It has been a luxury for me to have uninterrupted time to write letters—a rarity in Rio where the help needs me more than the girls, I sometimes think. Speaking of which . . .

Thank you for your questions about the girls. I feel I see them only at mealtimes here in the country as they are prowling out-of-doors the rest of the time. Didn't we do the same? Kiss those super blue Chilean skies for me. Here our skies are decorated with clouds. When they come like the purple-black of ripe fig skins, we know the storms they bring will be as damaging for those on land as on sea.

You asked me for stories concerning the girls. I think of one you would have liked as much as Benny. Both girls have been taking dancing lessons two blocks away from home in Rio with a wonderful American woman, plucked from the famous Rockettes in New York by her Brazilian doctor husband, Dr. Campos. We love them as a couple and for their individual talents. Anyway, as a sop to not putting our too young girls 'en pointe' (at the girls' insistence with too many movies in their heads!), Dorothy, as even her pupils call her, decided the girls could dance a duet

93

to 'The Blue Danube' at their end-of-year recital. We had blue tutus made and huge blue ribbons to put in their hair.

It became clear they had not had a dress rehearsal in the Copacabana hall with a darkened theatre and stage lights as when the real performance began, the girls must have been blinded by the lights at the apron of the stage. Everything, I guess, looked as black to them beyond the lights as towards the black backdrop curtain, so the girls faced backwards, away from the audience.

The orchestra, not knowing Dorothy Campos's choreography, started the music to those now-accursed five notes, and the girls did their beginning tour jetés until they heard the audience start to titter. On went the music, on went the girls, the titter grew to laughter. Suddenly, the front curtain went down, and we could hear Dorothy running out on stage to correct the girls, Arlette's scolding Denise with "I told you we were facing the wrong direction," and Denise's ever-so-common tears. I could picture Dorothy behind the scenes dabbing face powder to cover the traces of Denise's tears on her cheeks, and then, ta-da! the curtain went up and there were our darlings facing us to much applause. Credit to them, they finished their dance.

Benny, in the meanwhile, had started laughing so hard, that I'm sure the girls could hear his gulps of vain control over his hilarity. Fortunately, they know him and his love for little kids, his own in particular. Imagine! He calls children "les petits morpions, little brats." May all our problems be as passing as theirs, no matter how mortifying at the moment.

Love, Queta

* * *

On rainy days, we sit on the porch making corn dolls or playing "Cheat"—the new card game Sally has taught us where we let two packs of cards run through our fingers and onto our laps. We start out slowly, carefully leaving room for the other person to doubt us, then have to pay the penalty (more cards) if found to be wrong. It doesn't take long before we are dropping cards as fast as we can without the other person's being able to call "Cheat!" fast enough.

We listen to Tia Mildred's stories about her family. Since Arlette and I do not have many stories about our own, we borrow hers with the same hunger we feel for our food. Her stories make me feel as if I belong to a larger world, the American one in particular. Tia Mildred will not hurry her stories and, while she tells one, she gives us one of her many overly-detailed, if practical, food tips.

"Here, give me the knife. This is how you do it. You have to pour just a small amount of honey over the butter on your plate and then . . . see . . . here, *you* take the knife."

The task is simple but needs to be done well if it is to be effective, she assures us. "That's it, with the flat part of the blade, mash the butter and honey together. No, don't stir yet. The pieces of butter are still too big. That's it. No, I'm not going to finish it for you. You have lots of energy—I've seen you running in the fields."

But the knife soon is back in her hands. She does not like to give up control; besides, we'd never do any task well enough for her. Tia Mildred taps-taps the knife against the ingredients on the white enameled tin plate. When she stops and sits back from the table, we three girls take it as a cue to spread the fragrant, buttery-sweet concoction onto a toasted chunk of grey-doughed war bread made on the farm. We wolf it down, ask for more. "Piglet!" Tia Mildred scolds, then adds as if we were in a spelling bee, "P-i-g-l-e-t, Piglet!" She pushes up her high cheekbones into a reluctant smile and reaches for another slice to honey-butter for us while Mummy pours tea.

"Funny how it's important to try to keep the foods you've grown up with," Tia Mildred says. She sits straight-postured on a large rattan chair and pats the light brown curls that cap her head. "Poor Southerners who settled in Manaus never had time to miss their fancy cakes. Imagine Dom Pedro inviting the plantation owners who had lost everything in the Civil War to come farm in Brazil—worse yet, leading those people to think the jungle had fertile ground! Or their being so silly as to believe it in the first place. Honestly!" and here Tia Mildred vents exasperation with an explosive pshaw of *Pipocas!* Popcorn! something too insubstantial to grasp. "The settlers in the Amazon were too busy fighting dysentery, failing cotton crops and Indians attacks to miss pecans and Bourbon. Those who settled Villa Americana in São Paulo were luckier. They thrive there still."

I don't know about pecans, but I know Bourbon. I got sick on it once. Our parents had given a Manhattan cocktail party before going to dinner at the Rio Country Club one night and, as soon as they left, I ate all the maraschino cherries and orange slices from the bottom of the many glasses left lying around. The radio was still on, there was pretty classical music, Arlette wasn't interested and had gone back to our room. I took my time, played grown-up. The fruit, bloated in Bourbon and Angostura Bitters, tasted sweet going down, but I soon started to feel dizzy and sick. When our parents returned from dinner, they found me groggy on the living room and feeling ill. My breath must have given me away. With great kindness, they put me to bed and explained why I felt so awful. They didn't need to tell me not to repeat my prank.

There was something more to think about in what Tia Mildred had been saying. She had mentioned Dom Pedro, Brazil's last Emperor. Before coming to Jundiaí, our mother had taken Arlette and me to the Empire Museum in Petropolis. We drove in the *gasogenio* from Rio to the Organ Mountains where the Emperor's Palace stood about one hour away, the air getting cooler, the ferns more lush by the running stream below the hairpin turns of the road. Huge blue-winged butterflies colored the air.

We entered the old Portuguese-style palace of white-washed stucco, red-tiled roof and dark-framed windows and, without pausing, Mummy steered us into the dining room she had visited before. She stopped us at a glass case. "Girls, look at those candlesticks." The candlesticks formed a tall silver Baroque pair that didn't match. "Where have you seen two others like them?" she asked. On our buffet at home, we knew. It didn't occur to us to ask how we happened to have the same mismatched set in our own dining room; coincidences happen, we figured, never thinking about the journey those surely purloined items had taken to either a pawn shop or antique store or flea market, where our parents might have picked them up.

When Tia Mildred tells the story of Dom Pedro asking the American southerners to come settle in Brazil, I now imagine his inviting them to dinner first at this palace, and I picture the servants lighting the candles in the mismatched pair of candlesticks we Benzacars also have in Rio.

Through Tia Mildred's telling of stories about her past, Sally, Arlette and I have eaten our fill of honey-buttered bread and we are fidgeting. We will need to work up an appetite for our rice and beans and collards at supper, and the rain has lessened.

Vai embora! Go Away! She waves us good-by with a back-of-her-hand wave and laughs her tough guffaw. Sally is bounding down the steps, Arlette following. With honey on my hands and my heart in my mouth, in case Arlette and Sally decide I can't come, I, too, follow. In Jundiaí, there is space for us all.

CHAPTER EIGHTEEN

Jundiaí — More Stories, and Thinking Ahead

April, 1945

Dear Angie,

Don't faint. Truly, it's I, "Batty Buttons" from Oberlin. I wish you could see me now. A far cry from the girl who graduated with you in 1919. I am indulging in a fantasy so big, I live to make it come true. Last time we were together, we were closing out The Great War, and now we're in the midst of a second one that has come to haunt us in different ways. But before I tell you how, what I really want to say is that I hope when this slaughter is over, that we—Benny, our girls, Arlette and Denise, now 9 and 7—will come to the United States, the country you know I wanted to stay in. We will come to see you and your family. Benny has promised me.

This summer the girls and I are staying with American friends in a coffee plantation up in the hills to escape the heat and make the rations for sugar, in particular, last longer. In the city, the cooks insist on every imaginable sweet desert; here, we do most of the cooking ourselves. For us, life is splendid, beautiful, easy and makes the comparison with the lives of those in European cities seem more obscene. Our greatest challenge is getting the girls to drink KLIM, the whole powdered milk we get from the Americans, safer than the unpasteurized milk our often tubercular cows give, no fault of their own. The fact that KLIM spells

MILK backwards gets a laugh out of the girls, but doesn't make them drink the lumpy stuff with any more gusto.

Except for the rations, the war touches us little here except emotionally, of course. Our imaginations run gauntlets.

Benny has a younger step-sister, Jacqueline. She and Benny's mother and second husband live in Paris and, in Bordeaux, his father lives with his own second wife and child (Benny's parents separated when Benny and his two sisters were under age 8). The Bosches (no, I cannot be respectful) moved into the apartment in Paris and do everything to humiliate Jacqueline and Maman. When we meet, I shall be able to tell you reprisal stories.

Benny's father, a law professor at the University, and deputy mayor of Bordeaux, is in danger with the Vichy regime. We know little of what is going on despite the short wave radio. Letters from Europe are censored with those thick black lines drawn across words or whole sentences. To silence a voice seems the ultimate humiliation. We send occasional trivial news to Paris when we can find a reliable carrier. The Nazi net is cast wide, even to our shores. I fear exposure sending you this much.

I've done the unpardonable by writing on both sides of the onion skin. It will make it difficult for you—and any possible censors—to read.

My love to you and respectful greetings to your family, Queta

* * *

Over days of sun and rain, tea, KLIM, butter and honey, Tia Mildred and Mummy ravel and unravel their wool, recipes, and stories, but again the exchange is unequal. Mummy reveals little of her history while Tia Mildred is the unguarded story-teller. She's good at it and extends her family for me to adopt in pretend. She tells about her parents, parents she calls by their first names, Molly and Joe, something Arlette and I would never dare do.

"Molly was a southern belle to her fingertips. Tiny little thing. Her father was a great big horse rustler in Texas. He had moved to Georgia when he decided it was high time for his daughter to marry. He didn't give her any choice. Molly was fifteen when she married my father, Joe Coachman, and he'd barely cut his milk teeth. When Joe was sixteen, his own father had dropped him off in São Paulo, told him he should become a dentist pronto because 'I'm going to expect some money out of you.' Joe's brothers, who were younger, never had to work so hard. Joe was bull-headed enough to invent his way into dentistry and succeed. He'd take all day to tap a gold filling into your mouth with a little silver hammer he'd fashioned and, when he was finished, you had a work of art.

"Molly was sixteen when she gave birth to me. Never knew what it meant to be a mother. She was a resourceless little thing."

We never met Tia Mildred's father, but we know Molly, petite and porcelain-like, in white lace dresses and white lace parasol. I think of Molly, silent and calm in flouncy ankle-length whites as we have teas in Rio in the cool of the Wiseley's shaded dining room, or under rosewood trees in their garden, or on the white veranda of their Ipanema house, a house I remember for its uncluttered spaces, indoor and outdoor gardenias, cut-leaf philodendra and mango trees, and the wrap-around porch where we sat in the hot afternoons.

Molly is the only grandparent we know, and she does not fit the picture of anyone's parent. Calling Molly "Granny" is unthinkable. She comes to visit Tia Mildred and Sally in the afternoons because Mr. Wiseley does not care to find her in his home at night. He comes from a strict German family of farmers that settled in Ohio and doesn't take kindly, or at all, to frivolity. He has had to pay Molly's way out of casino debts in Rio and is resentful of her seemingly carefree presence. Tia Mildred understands him. She also understands that her lively mother never grew beyond a shortened girlhood.

"When I was six, Molly put me in a convent school and left me there. The nuns taught me to embroider, knit, crochet, hem, and if I didn't stitch things perfectly, they punished me. I've ripped up more miles of stitches!" Tia Mildred laughs at herself and I think this is what Mummy and Arlette mean when they tell me not to take things (myself) so seriously. Tia Mildred knows how not to. I keep listening. Maybe I'll learn.

"But the nuns were kind, too, she continues. "Or tried to be. One day, there was to be a carnival or circus, or maybe it was just a plain festival in Petropolis near the school. To attend, the nuns needed my parents' permission. For some reason, my parents said no. The nuns felt bad because they knew the event would be special for all us girls, so they contacted a near-by uncle, one of my father's younger brothers. Please, would he give permission for Mildred to go? For whatever reason, he also said no. In any case, I was the only student left at school that day. A nun stayed behind with me and offered to help me pray my way through the day, and so we knelt."

Tia Mildred laughs again, a full-hearted "Hah! Hah!" I feel sorry for her, but she does not feel sorry for herself. When I ask her why she doesn't, she answers: "Well?" as if to say what can one expect of the world?

I recall stories Mummy tells about her nuns, her teachers at Santiago College, how kind they were, how willing to enter into the children's ruse of an earthquake. I repeat this story often because it is one of the few I know about my mother, but it is already something. Compared to Tia Mildred's story about nuns, I know which ones I would have preferred.

Stories of earthquakes in Chile stay with me. If the land is unstable, my mother is as sure as myth.

To us, as well as to the farm workers, it is Tia Mildred's voice that instructs, not Mummy's: on the porch where they organize the meals for the day for us, and for the help; in the kitchen where our mothers wipe clean the oil-clothed table and rearrange the dented kettles, pots, pans, chipped bowls, pitchers, knives, spoons, forks; in contact with Pinote. Tia Mildred dominates. She is, after all, the *patroa da casa*, the lady of the house. She has been here before and she is the connection to the owners, the Gordinhos. "Yes, you're excused. Go play." We're excused, if Tia Mildred says so.

But it is Mummy who knows how to ride horses and how to accompany us on them, Mummy who seeks us truants in the wild when the weather turns bad, Mummy who knits sweaters for Pinote, his wife and their children. Tia Mildred knits, too, but with a perfection that stops her progress. Our mothers make passes at teaching us sewing as well as the constant knitting, but rain or shine, we prefer to be out of doors. I never hear our mothers argue about what they should let us do.

In the months of that transformative summer, one in which we have no cameras to record any of our moments of glee or self-revelation, the sounds layer and develop into an abbreviated natural Mass, a form I borrow from music, not religion:

Kyrie—Nature, have mercy on us (and She does)

Sanctus and Benedictus—sanctify and bless what we have seen in brick red earth, weathered blue, black and white skies, zebu humps; what we have touched of pig bristles, goat horns, horse manes, frog skins, lumpy water, slime and mud; what we have smelled of capim and stink bugs, air fresh from thunder storms, the mystery on our hands and from our bodies; what we have tasted of honey and sugar cane, coffee and boiled milk in the mornings, rice and black beans at night; what we have heard from the fazendero's soft baritone, Tia Mildred's tales, Mummy's susurrus, Arlette's laughter, Sally's decisive voice.

Gloria—for being alive, curious and seven.

Queta and Benny at their wedding in Santiago, Chile, 1933.

Mummy with Arlette, age 1.

Denise, Arlette, Sally Wiseley pouring tea in São Paulo backyard.

Arlette, age 6, dolled up for a party in Rio.

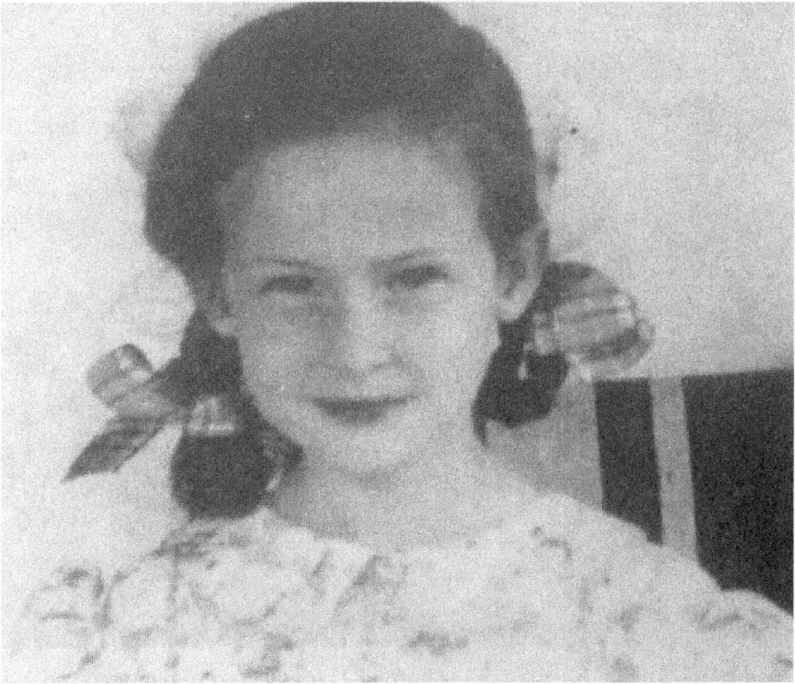

Denise, age 4, pigtails askew.

Denise, 6, Mummy, Arlette, 8.

Arlette, 11, Daddy, Denise, 8 — photo of Tante Dinah in background.

President Harry Truman in Brazil, 1947. Denise with outstretched arm.

Rear Admiral Andrew G. Shepard, our Uncle Andrew. He brought his light cruiser, the USS Cleveland to Rio after the War.

Laverne and Donald Murray, guardians to Arlette and me between 1949–1950 in Maplewood, New Jersey.

Louise Bernard Benzacar, Arlette's and my step-mother after 1950 in Montreal, Canada.

Our cousin, Nicole Rodrigues-Ely trying out the podium I will use for my short talk honoring my grandfather, her grand-uncle, Joseph Benzacar, in Bordeaux, 2014.

View of the Dois Irmãos in Gavea from the Ipanema beach we used to frequent.

PART THREE

After the War

CHAPTER NINETEEN

Caesura –
Rites of Passage

The New York Herald Tribune, May 8, 1945
"TODAY IS V-E DAY
Truman, Churchill, Stalin to Proclaim War's end;
Germans surrender at Eisenhower's Headquarters"

The newspaper is on the buffet next to the dining room table on which our parents are dancing. The war is over and there is no more normal.

Queridos, What a day!

I hope everyone is recording it. There is massive destruction to deal with, but at least there will be no more in Europe. I do not envy leaders with a conscience who live on knowing the numbers of young soldiers dead and maimed under their command. Had our family not left Europe, all of us might have died in one or other of the two world wars, but tonight, peaceful fireworks dug up from god knows where will be set off from ships in the Botafogo Bay with the Sugar Loaf as background. Invitations fly around from those who will have a direct view and we will take the girls with our American friends to their Embassy.

It came to light that Benny's brother-in-law, Andrew Shepard, was captain of the USS Cleveland from June, 1942 to August, 1944, a small cruiser that fought in the Pacific and destroyed four Japanese subs, according to one of the many stories beginning to be heard. The war in the Pacific continues, but we hear he may be coming to Brazil soon off-duty. Rumors? Truth? Let me know how you are celebrating.

We are thinking of you and sending love, Queta

*   *   *

"Uncle Andrew's ship is in town. We're going to meet him," our father tells Arlette and me. "Uncle Andrew is a Rear Admiral in the United States Navy," Daddy adds.

I don't know what that means except that from our father's tone of voice, Uncle Andrew must be important. What I understand is that Uncle Andrew is married to Tante Gilberte, the younger of my father's two sisters. She lives and stays in New York City no matter where Uncle Andrew sails.

Daddy takes us by trolley to the dock where the air is sweltering and still, the salty dampness so thick it mists the air. I feel as if I am breathing through a thick wet cloth that smells of all the fruity garbage floating in the water between the ships, but maybe my difficulty in breathing is because I'm nervous. We've never met any of our father's or mother's family and don't know what to expect, or what they will expect of us.

We see Uncle Andrew's ship tied up alongside the dock. As we approach, we read *USS Cleveland* on the prow. The ship is so big from near that it hides the purple green mountains defining Guanabara Bay behind it. I love the silhouettes of these mountains. They give seasonal reds, yellows and blues from the flamboyant trees or mimosas, or jacaranda trees, and seem to echo the singing and *batucada* rhythms of the people on board the ferries going back and forth to Niteroi or to Paquetá. It doesn't take strangers to tell me Rio is beautiful. I know it is, but this morning, I have to admit the ship has its own beauty. It looks and smells freshly painted in a comforting medium grey that absorbs some of the bright light reflected off the harbor. And there is the excitement of stepping on a gangplank with its cross slats so that our feet don't slide back down the steep incline. At the top, waiting for us, is Uncle Andrew. We hear a piercing whistle as the sailors salute him.

He is dressed in a bright white Navy uniform that looks so starched, I wonder his knees can move. His hair is cut short and graying, his lips are thin and his jaw is square, as if he could be very strict, but it is his eyes crinkled in smiles that tell us he is kind. He welcomes us at the top of the gangplank and lets us come on board his ship that smells of linoleum waxes and brass polish. He lets us explore the ship, makes sure we pay attention to stepping over each high transom of the steel doors hooked open, and ensures we inhale the scent of freshly-baked bread and clean laundry coming from below-deck.

The sailors stand straight and salute when Uncle Andrew goes by. Arlette and I pretend the salute is for us and try to hide our grins as we alternately gawk at and show-off in front of the sailors in their bell-bottom uniforms and jaunty white hats. I am dark-haired, paunchy, and shy. Arlette is nearly eleven and sunny, our friends tell me repeatedly. With Uncle Andrew's permission, the young, handsome sailors give us some American delicacies: Hershey bars that melt quickly in the Rio sun, and oh-so-pink bubble gum. I don't admit to not liking the taste of either, but I love the comics written in English that wrap round the pieces of Double Bubble.

Harry S. Truman, the new President of the United States, comes to Brazil. The American Embassy is having a party and all of us students at the American School have been invited to come to meet him. A picture in one of the American papers a friend sends to us weeks later shows Arlette and me smiling, our arms outstretched to reach for his hand. He, in turn, is smiling widely at our circle of faces. Truman comes, but then many of our friends go: my friend Helen Norman goes back to England, my godparents go back to France, Arlette's godfather, Uncle Rudy, returns to China where he worked for Otis before the war. Many of our American friends go home, including Sally and her parents.

In December of 1945, we ourselves leave Rio, but only for summer holiday. Mummy is preparing us for a dream of hers: to get to the United States. She and our father do everything to make memorable the trip itself.

"This is the first ship to leave Rio since the war ended," our father tells us. "It belonged to the French but then the Argentines took it over. It's called the *Rio Jachal*."

The day we finally see the ship, its lack of guns and torpedo ports clearly show it is no longer a military vessel, but neither is it a tourist ship the way we know the Cunard Line ships are, the ships we've seen our American friends leave on, and it is nowhere near as clean as Uncle Andrew's. Our walk up the gangplank at the Rio harbor is followed by a walk down narrow, steep stairs below deck where we squeeze together in a cabin of grey painted metal walls. Four bunks and a tiny bathroom crowd together. Cockroaches compete for space and win it. We spend most of the trip on deck.

As the ship draws farther away from our waving friends, the well-known outlines of the Sugar Loaf, the statue of Christ on the Corcovado, and Gavea's Two Brothers, fog over in a blue-to-purple haze. The ship picks up speed, dives into swells, and the steady thunk-thunk of the engines becomes our pedal point. Sea gulls give way to dolphins that race us on either side of the prow, and flying fish land on deck with a whack. We throw them back into the sea whose lulling rhythmic constancy I love.

The air is breezy and hot, hotter two days later as we round the hump of Brazil and pump through the muddied waters where the

Amazon River gives up its tons of stolen earth as a gift from the gods. We continue north.

"King Neptune requests your presence on deck tomorrow at noon," reads a notice on the ship's bulletin board. "Adults may accompany children."

"What's this about, Mummy?"

"We'll see. Wear your bathing suits."

What does she know that we don't? There's nothing on the notice about bathing suits. Who is King Neptune? He sounds like Santa Claus, a creature that belongs in a world made up by grown-ups for children. Santa operates in the northern hemisphere mostly, but he comes to Rio, too. From our dining room balcony Arlette and I shout "Merci, Papa Noël," for our Christmas presents because our father tells us to.

"Who is King Neptune?"

"He's the King of the oceans."

"Why is he boarding the Rio Jachal?"

"Be patient, Denise. You'll see tomorrow."

And then, there he is: skinny, muscular like the athletic *maxixi* dancers we see on the beach, barefoot, tall, with a false white beard, a trident in hand, a white tunic falling from his shoulders. He does not look like King Babar, the only king that comes to mind, and I find him unsettling. A sailor carries a bucket with a paint brush inside and stands next to the King.

"Line up, those who would be part of my Court," the King booms in his deep-voiced Portuguese. The seven of us children line up. The grown-ups are smiling. This is their game and we need to join in.

"Have you been good?" King Neptune thunders at the first child in line.

"Yes," says the boy who had been anxious to be first but now looks as if he'd prefer to be last.

"Are you sure?" the King growls.

"Yes," repeats the boy.

"Then you shall have one lash only." And with that, King Neptune picks up the brush and sloshes a dark liquid over the boy's chest. He stumbles over to the line of sailors who look amused and welcome him into King Neptune's Court.

"Next," commands the King.

The second boy gets brush strokes across his chest, face and arms despite his guarantee he'd been good but, by then, the scent of chocolate that lies melting in the bucket reaches our nostrils.

"More lashes!" becomes the cry by the time Arlette and I are accepted into the court. We are very pleased with our new regal state.

The sailors bring a cake decorated with sea creatures on it and by the time we are through eating the cake, drinking sweet fruit juices and licking the chocolate from our bodies, we are a feast for ants.

The Rio Jachal's swimming pool has been constructed for its first batch of tourists, but it holds no more than three children at a time. The deck slopes towards a drain and that's where those of us who aren't thrown into the pool stand when the sailors take hoses to us all, swab us as clean as the wood we stand on. That night at dinner, we receive a certificate for crossing the Equator, another transposition in our lives.

Trinidad is our first port of call for a day. Our parents guide us from the ship onto a horse cart to clip-clop round the beauty of the capital, Port of Spain. Hibiscus, gardenias, bougainvilleas, banana and mango trees pop back into view. We could have been in a calèche in Paquetá, one of the islands we four love to visit in Rio's harbor, and maybe this is our parents' way of telling us things aren't so different elsewhere. Keeping time with the clip-clop of the horses, our father is singing the Charles Trenet song *Un fiacre allait trottinant* but, as usual, he is changing the words to tell us that when the horse trots, it farts—as we can hear and smell. The familiarity of the ride and his singing are comforting and it's nice to laugh together.

Back on board that night, we steer towards Willemstad, Curaçao, the Dutch Island in the Netherlands Antilles that had been so carefully guarded during the war. It had oil fields, refineries and a good harbor for the transportation of this military blood. The waters around it had been multiply mined, and our ship goes slowly.

"Arlette, Denise, wake up! Keep your pajamas on and come on deck. Quickly."

It is not like our mother to wake us at 3 am. What's wrong? Are we in trouble? Have we hit a mine? We realize the engines of the boat have gone silent. Our mother's voice is the only propellant.

She drags us by the hand onto the deck and says: "Look up,"

We look into a night sky with so many shooting stars criss-crossing, they whiten the dark dome like a badly erased blackboard. The stars fly across the skies, burn themselves out mid-air, or seem to fall into the sea to the rhythm of an accelerating metronome. The show doesn't end. Our necks and eyes tire before the heavens do and just when we think we might creep back into bed to wonder over what we have seen, Mummy stops us: "Not yet. Look over there." Her finger points to what seems like a thin necklace of pearls strung across a path in the sea. The ship's engines restart and as we get nearer, we realize these pearls are anchored on either side by land. We are seeing Queen Juliana's draw bridge which is opening for us.

"This is the first time they have allowed lights on the bridge since the end of the war. We are the first to see it."

When we wake in port the next morning, the thick scent of petroleum distillation fouls the air, makes me gag. There is no way to escape except by leaving the island. Our parents take us for a walk away from the loading areas where the hoses transfer the oil into the ships' cargo holds, but even diluted, the stink is potent. Our own ship takes on this black 'liquid gold,' the sailors call it, what every business needed so desperately during the war and I wonder why anyone could ever like it.

We have one last port of call: Havana, Cuba. The breakers are huge as we pass the Moro Castle and come into the harbor surrounded by beautiful stone walls. We will have four days here and our mother is marking time. "Wait until you see New York," she tells us.

To fill the time, she takes us shopping in a department store, something Arlette and I never do in Rio because we have no need to. Outside of buying food and *tamancos* in the markets, our clothes are made at home. Even shoes are often hand-me-downs, American ones, if we're lucky.

The three of us stand on the black and white squares of polished marble in one of Havana's elegant stores. The crystal chandeliers spark prisms of light that reflect off the mirrored walls so that I feel as if I have entered some kind of fairy tale that keeps repeating itself into infinity. My mother must sense my awe and does not want me to fall prey to fantasy. "Wait until you see New York," she reminds me in a voice I do not want to hear, at least, not right now. I do not want to hurry from this place to a city unknown to me even if my all-knowing mother says so. I still have the perfume samples to analyze as I nose my way from one resplendent counter to the next. We have stepped out of a natural landscape full of its own floral exuberance into this indoor marvel. I see a wave of silk stockings artistically arranged over a mannequin's arm blow in and out at us in the puffs of a slowly rotating wall fan. I know silk stockings are still a luxury in December of 1945 and compare this glut with the single pairs the Callahan sisters secreted for Mummy in the rolled up pages of *The Brooklyn Eagle*. I recall my mother's smile as the stockings fell lightly into her hand, and hear her whispered private 'thank you' to them, and to the Americans who made it through for us constantly during the war.

So, I think to myself, if stockings in Havana come from the USA, and New York is part of the USA, maybe our mother is right. Maybe New York is just as good as (if not better than) Havana, but I want another day to wander with my father into the area where the smell of rum and coke fills the cobble-stoned streets and where music hip-wiggles from every bar and restaurant, and I want another chance to eat one more coconut ice cream served in the half shell of a coconut. And could he take us to that place in Havana where he lived in 1925 when they had the hurricane that made roofs fly horizontally across the landscape? He had loved Havana and I do, too. I don't want this stop-over to end.

We reach New York early in the morning on January 11th, 1946. The sky is grey and the buildings are fogged over; the famous skyline is hidden from us. The ship drops anchor outside Ellis Island waiting for doctors to come to us on launches and board ship so they can inspect us for coughs, colds, measles, and all the other diseases we should not bring into a new country. We know our parents have all the passports and health papers and, I think, if the doctor insists on seeing proof of vaccination, I can show him the scar behind my left calf from the smallpox vaccination I had. In secret, I am relieved I don't have a cough. Whatever would they do with someone who is sick? If someone is taken off the ship, I do not see it. I do see the Statue of Liberty wrapped in cold vapor.

Hours later, I hear the anchor come up and we head for a berth on the docks of New York's west side. We disembark into a space that is like a light-filled cavern and go to stand beneath the overhead signs with letters of the alphabet on them. We go to B for Benzacar and line up with the other passengers in their hats and coats, scuff alongside our collective steamer trunks and suitcases to be checked by immigration and custom's officials. Our father has rehearsed this process with us carefully. "Never, ever lose your papers," he has said to us repeatedly in French, but I don't worry about my papers as Mummy has them. We are to behave, Arlette and I. Somehow, we have borrowed coats we can take back to Rio, but I am cold. I shuffle left-right, left-right behind the others and think we look like unimaginative dancers swaying in a line together in a black and white movie.

Thanks to our mother, we have English to answer the doctor, the customs and immigration officials. It never occurs to us what it would be like not to speak the language, but with language, we have everything.

Our disembarkation has taken all morning and then, suddenly, we are on the city side of the officers. We are free to move, find a taxi, go wherever we wish. The Grandgérards, who had been transferred back to New York right after the war, have promised to pick us up. Mr. Grandgérard—Oncle Charles to us—was Daddy's boss in Rio. They got along well because of their French backgrounds, but 'C.P.,' as he was known by his first two initials, has lived in New York City and China and Japan, too. He tells Arlette and me *Ikimasho!* which means to hurry up in Japanese. He makes us laugh here as he used to make us laugh when he would swing from one tree branch to another along the lane of the Rio Country Club. His wife, Tante Chrisje, came from Holland. She is the one with smallpox scars on her face, which is otherwise quite pretty. She looked after Arlette and me in Rio sometimes when our mother had appointments to keep that we couldn't go to.

The Grandgérards lived on Moro da Viuva, Widow's Hill. From its big windows, we could look across the Bay of Botafogo to the Sugar Loaf Mountain with its funicular, but my clearest memories of being with her center around not having to eat the hard-boiled egg yolk she floated in the tomato soup, and of sitting on the hall floor watching the numbers of the elevator rise and fall waiting for our mother's return while Arlette was busy inside their apartment being agreeable.

Here in New York City, as promised, we are hugging each other. "We're going to Child's for pancakes," Oncle Charles says noticing we are shivering. We have exchanged tropical heat and bright colors for grey skies and snow pock-marked with coal dust. He hails two cabs, one for himself, our father, Arlette and me; the other for Tante Chrisje, our mother, and all the baggage that is to be dropped off at the Park Avenue Hotel on 38th and Park Avenue. The women will join us at Child's, four blocks away on 42nd Street. "Wait until you see Grand Central Station," Oncle Charles says like a variant to our mother's "Wait until you see New York."

The pancakes appear at out table. Arlette loves the thick flat cakes and the war-time sugar syrup that comes with them, but I miss the thinner crêpes like the one our father stuck up on the kitchen ceiling. I want nothing more than to dunk a piece of tough war-grey bread into my father's cup of strong café-au-lait he drinks at our dark rosewood dining room table in Rio. He tries to repeat the treat at Child's red Formica-topped table, but the bread I put into his drink dissolves, and the lukewarm liquid is nothing like coffee or tea. I am ashamed because Arlette loves the pancakes and I know I should, too. She is full of smiles, her blue eyes crinkle in pleasure and our friends tousle her blond curls (no one fears that she will be called a little German here). I sense my mother's impatience with my bad manners, my father's more understanding regret that, once again, I am not measuring up to the child they wish I might be.

"Play with the snow," our friends encourage when we leave Child's. They pick up a handful from the top of a letter box, and I do the same. It is icy and cold, and I have no gloves. I smile to please them, plunge my hands into the snow and ice my wrists. I quickly lift my hands up into my coat sleeves where the snow melts unpleasantly.

For the first time, I question my mother's judgment. What does she like about New York? But I begin to understand when we step into the drug store next to Child's and there is something that sends me into an animal frenzy it pleases me so: the smell of an American drug store. As if I were back by the perfume counter in Havana's elegant department store, I sniff my way like a dog through the shelves of soaps and perfumes, fill my lungs and brain with odorants and deodorants. The grown-ups can leave me there for hours if they want to shop. I will not stray.

The only thing that makes this experience better is the next day when we discover a Woolworth's on Fifth Avenue across from the New York Public Library with its beautiful lions guarding the steps. Woolworth's has the same soaps and lotions I discovered in Havana, but it also has an escalator marked "Otis." Our father had told us Otis was installing the first escalator in a Sears Roebuck building in Rio before we left. Arlette and I felt cheated not to discover the moving staircase there, but New York gives it to us.

"It's time to go, girls."

"Once more, just once more—an up and a down."

"You will have to try skating," the Grandgérards say to an activity so unimaginable for Arlette and me, that it has no element of fear in it. They take pictures of us skating at a small rink near the hotel and at Rockefeller Center. With our borrowed clothes, Arlette and I look like the European war orphans we now see in Movietone reels but, except for our toes in ill-fitting skates, we are warm and think skating is fun.

We meet Uncle Andrew again. He comes to pick us up at the hotel and this time he is not in his Admiral's uniform. He is going to take us by cab to where he and Tante Gilberte live in an apartment on the third floor facing north on East 57th Street. There is not much traffic this far east, and as soon as our taxi pulls up outside their apartment building, Uncle Andrew purses his skinny lips and produces what sounds like the bosun's whistle we heard on board ship. They arrange to keep their windows open so that Tante Gilberte can keep track of our arrival. This is the first time we have met a real blood relative on either side of the family, and it is our aunt's voice we first hear through that window.

"COCO! TAFFY! TAIS-TOI! FOUS-MOI LE CAMP!" she yells at her barking dogs in the background. Those familiar words prove to us that she is our father's sister; she uses his same vocabulary.

We take the elevator with a metal accordion door that is heavy to open and clangs shut. The elevator bounces to a stop on the third floor and, when we have opened the gate, we can scarcely get out for the two brown and white cocker spaniels that jump and drool all over us, push us back into the small elevator. From the door to their apartment, Tante Gilberte shouts commands to have them re-enter the apartment, but the dogs continue to trip us up. My father does not like being in elevators (a Schindler, not as good as Otis, our father reminds us) and is pushing us into the dogs to get us onto terra firma. We find the dogs noisy and disagreeable, and I think how few dogs I see indoors in Rio. People there keep monkeys and birds, cats to chase the rats, and guard dogs, but not pets like these.

With inching steps, we enter their small apartment. Tante Gilberte forgets about the dogs that have settled on their own cushions on the couch, and she concentrates on us. She is full of hugs and clearly happy to welcome her brother, his wife, and their daughters. She holds her brother, whom she calls "Jean," at arm's length the better to look at him and, as I see them side by side, I realize she looks like our father. They share dark hair and big noses and she laughs as she realizes the resemblances. She has not seen him since he left France after the First World War. She was in her late teens then and had not yet made her own way out of Paris, a divorce from a Spaniard who beat her up, or married the wonderful Uncle Andrew. But these histories we find out later.

Tante Gilberte has laid a table with a cloth she embroidered, home-made cakes and cookies and tea, stronger than the coffee we had at Child's. We can add real milk into it, not KLIM.

The chair she sits on is surrounded by baskets full of knitting yarns, the source of the wonderful knitted dresses she made for our dolls in Rio.

The next day, Tante Gilberte introduces us to the Marx brothers in "A Day at the Races" at a small movie theatre near their apartment. As wonderful as the film is, Tante Gilberte's laughter—so loud and unchecked—infects the whole theatre. The audience laughs as much at her sobs of joy as at the antics on screen. I am a bit embarrassed, but then realize I am laughing as hard as she, only I don't know how to laugh so loud.

We meet our father's relatives in Rochester, New York, too, and connect Tante Dinah to her picture over our sofa in the living room in Rio. We meet her husband Harry Windholz, a GI who fought in France and was gassed by the Germans in the First World War. He speaks in a raspy whisper and gives Arlette and me each a Brownie box camera he can buy because he works for Eastman Kodak. We play with their son, Alain, the first real cousin we've met. He is dark haired and handsome, older than Arlette and I are, and we both have immediate crushes on him.

There are two great aunts, sisters to our father's mother, who is the only one left in France. I think they are amused that we speak French and English and Portuguese. They ask us to say things in one or another of the languages. Tante Jeanne is as tall and skinny as Tante Vette is short and round. Tante Jeanne pulls back her white hair in a chignon. She is much taller than her husband, Jean Garibaldi, who is bald and endearing, and who, years later, will inhabit for me the body of Nabokov's Pnin. Jean is a wine merchant, finds the humor in selling New York State wines after selling Italian and French ones.

Tante Vette is married to Arthur See, the financial secretary of the Eastman School of Music. He walks with the help of eight pounds of steel braces. Like my Chilean friend, Ursula, in Rio, he had polio. Tante Vette and Uncle Art open their libraries and record collections to us, but we are not there enough time to take advantage of these gifts. In less than five years, I will be spending all my time immersed in their books and music and thanking them for caring for Arlette and me. Their house on Cobb's Hill Drive has beautiful French glass doors that open up onto Highland Park and give me the feeling I am outside most of the time. Apart from all the books and music, their house is full of cats and I will come to think of Tante Vette as another Colette, the French writer.

And then, finally, we go to see our mother's roommate in Oberlin, Angie Sands, our mother's real reason for wishing to return to the United States. Angie lives in Skaneateles, New York.

To get there, we take a train from New York City, and enter Grand Central Station. I feel as if I've become weightless and can rise above this enormous shiny cave to look down at the desk and a clock in the center. Staircases go every which way, and there are multiple numbered doors in rows along one side of the station leading to the tracks of trains going to different places. The voice announcing the arrivals and departures echoes in the huge hall and brings me back to earth. I want to cover my ears against the ricocheting noise, and pray not to be lost here. And then I focus on the very large photograph rising above one of the walls of the station. In letters that can be read from any point in the station, I read what I learned when Uncle Harry gave us our Brownie cameras, "Kodak," printed across the upper left-hand corner. The rest of the photo shows a series of shallow transparent waterfalls that curve around rocks and ferns in sprays of sunlight. The scene looks cool. Almost falling into the water is a huge dark blue and white tube of peppermint lifesavers open at one end so I can see a white circle with a hole in the middle. Mummy tells me it is a candy. I have never tasted one, but clearly I should. The scene calms me down from having to travel to meet yet another stranger, who is not even a family member, and I don't notice the train ride, what we eat, or anything else until the train stops in Skaneateles.

Angie comes to fetch us in her car. We notice her car does not have the big coal canisters on the back of it the way cars do in Rio, and that there is no room for her husband to come, too, so we are alone with her. She gives my mother a hug and ignores the rest of us.

"I was so surprised when you called, I'm sure I swallowed my cigarette; at least, I never found it and we didn't go up in smoke."

I am curious to see someone who would do that, but have little image of this woman, the one our mother had spoken of so often. She is like my mother in height, but whether or not she is fat, thin, blue-eyed, dark-haired, I cannot say. She drives with her back to Arlette and me, her hair is under a hat, and when we arrive at her house, she melts into it.

The house is not like any other I have seen. It is large with lots of small dark rooms inside, spaces for our mothers to be together. I hear them talking, but it's as if Angie is always out of view. She orders her two young children to entertain Arlette and me, and entertainment means going out into the snow and cold to sled. Her husband and our father are thrown together to keep each other company. They are so different, I know my father will have little to say to him and feel sorry for both men.

It is not long before my feet are icy in borrowed galoshes, and I cannot put politeness before my discomfort. I limp my way back uphill to the Sands' house to warm up and leave Arlette and the other kids to continue the same up-down of sledding, but soon after I have closed the door of the house—with me on the warm side—Arlette comes in, equally cold and unhappy.

"Put your feet up on the radiator," Angie tells us from the other room. We unclip the cold rubber galoshes, pull off our wet shoes with difficulty and pain, and put our white-toed feet on the too-hot rungs of the radiator. We cannot keep them there. The contrast of temperatures is too extreme, but we try on and off for twenty minutes before our mother comes in and suggests we take a bath in warm water, not hot. Had she done this when she was in Oberlin? I hate this experience.

We have no more in common with Angie's kids than our fathers do with each other, and they are as confused as Arlette and I are about what to do next. When can we leave? I know we spend a night with them but don't remember how and where in the house we do. I hope Mummy had enough of a good time that she doesn't want to go back for another visit.

There is one more stop our father wants us to make in New York City before we have to sail home.

"She asked us, Queta. I think we should go."

Daddy is talking about Diane W., an American woman we met on our voyage on board the Rio Jachal. Since Daddy and I were on deck more often than Arlette and Mummy, who were sea-sick, I got to see more of her. She would come over to be with us when we stood at the prow. She dressed like a Hollywood actress with bright red lipstick and matching finger nail polish. She wore high-heeled sandals and I could see that even her toe nails were painted the same bright red. Her dresses buttoned all the way down the front and either she wore a blue dress with white collar and buttons, or a white dress with blue collar and buttons. She was the color of the American flag.

She began to annoy me by never leaving us alone, and she would put her hand on Daddy's arm, or link her arm around his. One day of heavy swells she pressed herself up to our father and said very close to his mouth: "Oh, Benny, I feel so sea-sick. What should I do about it?"

"Go right to the front of the ship and look straight down," he said.

"I tried that, Daddy," I told him later, "and it was awful. I was scared and it made the waves seem bigger." He smiled, patted my head and said nothing.

We didn't see her again until we reached New York. As we were leaving the ship, Diane came up to our father and said: "You must all come to have a post-war celebration dinner at my apartment. I live on Park Avenue," and she gave her address and her hand to Daddy, as if he were supposed to kiss it. He didn't.

"I feel badly about the way I treated her," he tells our mother, and Arlette in front of me. Why and what had he told them about what had happened? I didn't think he had treated Diane badly except for making her look straight down into the ocean from the prow of the ship. I thought she had been a pest and didn't like her, or the way she was around our father.

"We have one more day in New York. Diane's apartment is not far from where Percy lives," he adds, addressing us girls. "We can visit them first as they have asked us several times to come over, and then go on to dinner at Diane's."

Percy is the son of one of the heads of Otis in New York City. He is older than Arlette, keen to show off, and we all like one another.

Arlette and I are in another kind of paradise at Percy's. He and his mother allow us to jump on his fancy bed while he prepares smelly concoctions with his chemistry set. "You want blue smoke?" he asks, then produces it in a puff of acrid haze. He then pours other liquids from his test tube into a small beaker. "There, yellow!" and yellow smells worse than blue. We collapse in laughter at his daring. There do not seem to be any limits until we ask if we might do some of the mixing ourselves. "No, too dangerous," he says.

We leave Percy's, unhappy to be pulled from real magic, and I am not anxious to see Diane W. again. Mummy isn't either, I can tell. She is not trying to make small talk for us, and she is not speaking to our father.

We reach Diane's apartment house and are ushered into a fancy elevator of parqueted woods we see on floors in Rio, but never on walls. An elevator man takes us up to her apartment on the 14th floor while Arlette and I try not to have giggles at how very serious he looks in a uniform like the man wears in the advertisement for Philip Morris cigarettes we saw in Times Square.

The elevator door opens right into a circular hallway full of mirrors and a red round couch in the middle of the room. Something tall grows out of the middle, but I have not seen a plant like it before.

Diane swishes in to greet us dressed in a long white satin dressing gown and matching loose trousers underneath. She wears strapless sandals on her feet. ("They're called 'mules'," Arlette shares in a whisper when she catches me staring at them and understands our shared fascination with American shoes of any sort.) The same red nails from on board ship come out to greet us with Diane's handshake. "So glad you could come."

The contrast between her and our mother has me stifling giggles again. Mummy is Mummy—short, shapeless, soft, cushiony, comfortable. She wears the kind of floral dress she wears in Rio and stocky shoes that at least don't lace up. I can see she is angry, deeply angry, and I want to give her a hug and tell her it is all make-believe, like in Hollywood, but in the movies it's fun and here, in real life, it isn't.

"You must see my bedroom," Diane says in a surprise first sentence.

Here is another red, round room, but it is only the round vermillion bed that makes it seem so. Why does she want a mirror on the ceiling? I hate the fussy room and want to run from it as if spider threads stinking of Percy's sulphur experiments will catch on my arms if I don't.

"I've made an early dinner for the girls," she says, and saves us from staying longer in the bedroom. We enter a very formal dining room full of furniture that has gold at the ends of everything, and sit down at table as she directs. Diane sits at the head of the table with Daddy at her right, where we know guests of honor are placed. Our mother is at the end of the table opposite Diane. Arlette and I are to our mother's right, opposite our father. The table is set with lots of silverware, sparkling glasses and gold-rimmed plates.

Diane motions to a Chinese man. "You can start dinner now," she says and, moments later, the fellow comes in with scrambled eggs and ketchup in a platter that does not look as if it would feed us all.

We four Benzacars fall silent. Is this the dinner? For whom are the scrambled eggs? Is she feeding Arlette and me first while the grown-ups await something special, like what our mother and Raimunda prepare for us and guests alike? And if the eggs are only for us girls, what happens when the proper dinner is brought in? Can we eat it, too? Or do we have to sit there and watch? Our parents warn about food shortages still existing after the War, but Diane doesn't look as if she needs to worry about a shortage of anything. We all are confused, but whatever is going on is unacceptable to my mother who stands up from the table and says: "We're leaving."

Oh, glory! What bad manners, and how wonderful! I know not to laugh, but I am so pleased that our mother spoke up, that I want to whoop out loud. I feel Arlette does, too, so we don't look at each other. What does Daddy feel? I think he must feel kind of stupid and embarrassed, but I don't care. He's the only one who wanted to come, and being here has bewildered us. Mummy is not objecting to the food, we know that. She is objecting to Diane going after Benny, even in front of his wife and children (Why on earth show that tasteless bedroom?); she is outraged Diane thought she might impress us with her fancy stuff; she is furious over any insinuation we appeared inferior to Diane. As a respectful and appreciative manager of help in Rio, Mummy is sorry for the poor Chinese servant. He did not look too comfortable serving an inexplicably small portion of eggs. Mostly, Mummy is disgusted.

It doesn't take long for Arlette and me to shake hands with the red nails again and to say thank you to Diane. We follow our mother to the elevator, for which she already has rung.

I feel the elevator man is dying to ask questions, but no one in a Philip Morris suit in the movies ever does. The evening is not lost. I have learned a lot about at least one grown-up.

After two months, we return to Rio aboard the *SS Scania*, a Swedish freighter that takes only us four as passengers. Mummy and Arlette are as pale as the Skaneateles snow with sea-sickness. Our father and I roam the decks, pick up flying fish which we put in the tub of our stateroom so Arlette and Mummy can see. They scream for us to take them away. We round Cape Hatteras in a hurricane and all the dishes on board ship break. We eat cereal and milk from boxes the rest of the trip. We re-cross the Equator, this time with no party, but by now, we already have our certificates, so it doesn't matter.

Knowing our love for the sea, the sailors tie my father and me to stanchions while we dip and shudder out of waves that cover us. The ride to Rio never calms down. When we near the oh-so-beautiful Guanabara harbor, the captain commands Arlette and me to sit at the base of the mast and look up. The tip arcs left to right around 100 degrees in the swells that carry us in (and normally would have carried Arlette indoors), but the beauty of the Guanabara Bay, the mountains, the taste of salt air and the scent of heated land keep both of us on deck listening to the seagulls and pointing out every familiar landmark to quell our *saudades*, our longing. The Christ statue on the Corcovado is there with open arms as if waiting to hug us. We are back home.

CHAPTER TWENTY

Patience

April, 1946

Chère Margot,

I feel unmoored, but I don't know where to dock anymore. Knowing how happy I was in Oberlin way back when, it will be no surprise to you to learn how happy I was again to be back in the United States. It was different to see it through the girls' eyes, never mind Benny's. His recollections of his stay in the U.S. date from when he came away forever from France in 1923, a green engineer with nothing to do and not much English to do it with.

I'm not sure you ever heard the story of how he ended up in South America, though you remember him well from Santiago. When he reached the wharves of New York, an American GI friend from his ambulance-driving days in the war met him and suggested Benny go train with Otis Elevators in Yonkers; so, that's what he did, straight off the boat in his limited and accented English, and with Otis he has stuck. Two years in Chicago on the catwalks of the Hippodrome, where he loved every bird's eye view of Pavlova and Nijinsky, two years in Havana (the best years of his bachelor life), then his tours of duty in Buenos Aires, Santiago, São Paulo and Rio. The last three you know about.

The girls enjoyed meeting his relatives who were darling with them—as amused as curious about these metamorphosing creatures who spoke French to them, if they wanted, but usually English. The girls glimpsed scintillas of Benny's sparky past, loved hearing the story of his sister's sic'ing on him a small dog he was terrified of. He was four at the time. He ran off with the dog pell-mell on his heels. Benny—or Jean, as they call him from youth—managed to skid into their father's studio, lock the door, and take out the key. When the girls taunted him from the other side of the door and took turns putting their eyes to the keyhole, they reported his standing on his father's desk, arm across his chest Napoleon style, and shouting "Apportez-moi un lion." Safe to say, they had no lion to bring.

The other story that impressed them was one he told on himself about stealing some of his father's law books just before he left for the United States to buy himself a pair of nifty wing-back brown and white shoes he had seen some dandy wearing in an American magazine.

The girls looked wide-eyed in disbelief and gulped a nervous laugh. "Wasn't he mad?" they asked about their heretofore unknown grandfather.

Benny went for his cigarette holder and scratch pad to make them a picture and nothing more was said. We are a maddeningly discreet bunch.

And, yes, I did have a wonderful time in Ohio catching up with Angie and my Oberlin days. As with any intense and recovered time, it was difficult to know where to begin, what to leave out, what to expand, explain, make light of, or where to connect on whatever intellectual interest we had in college then. It didn't help that our children kept running in and out—frozen, as it happened—from miserable times sledding in the cold. And so, the time passed quickly and we parted with even more longing to re-establish what we both know never can be the same. Benny and Angie's husband tolerated each other politely, but that was all. What could anyone expect? And American cuisine is not Benny's taste. We all are spoiled, and the war shortages still showed.

It's always frustrating to think: "If only I had asked about..." or "Why didn't I make that connection sooner?" or "How did it happen that we all got together in the first place?"

"*What brought you to Oberlin?" Angie asked, wanting only to re-hear what she already knew: 'A recruit from the wonderful college came to Chile and seduced me—not in body, but in mind (a college founded on educating women!), though I might have welcomed the former as well. We weren't such innocents, after all.'*

I shall try to ramble on further in my next letter, but planning dinner is a welcome distraction as I re-enter our Brazilian world. The girls are so glad to be back, like puppies tracing their scents, bounding from one familiar taste to another, pawing their books, skidding barefoot on the wonderfully cleaned and polished floors Agenor treats us to. Not bad.

My love, as ever,

Queta

* * *

It is very windy the day Mummy and I are on the big front porch of our house in Ipanema. Often she sings me songs, medleys she learned when she was in college at Oberlin, a song I heard her sing when we were visiting Angie Sands in Skaneateles:

Oh Hell . . . Oh Hell . . . Oh Helen to be mine,
Your feet, your feet, your features are divine,
I swear, I swear,
I don't want to get well, I don't want to get well,
I'm in love with a beautiful nurse!
Early in the morning, night and noon,
He would row, row, row, row, row along the river
He would row, row, row, row, row, a kiss he'd give her,
He'd kiss her now and then; she would tell him when,
Then she'd say: 'Sit down! Sit down!'
Down by the stream on Morgan Street
There I shall anchor my sailboat fleet,

Safe in the dark, we will embark,
For there's a long, long trail a-winding
Into the land of my dreams,
Where the nightingales are singing...
Kuh-Kuh-Kuh-Katie, my beautiful Katie,
You're the only guh-guh-guh-girl that I adore,
When the moo-moon shines over the cow shed,
I'll be waiting at the kih-kih-kih-kitchen door.

The air is hot and dry, like my throat, which is sore. Mummy has tied a Kotex soaked in alcohol inside a handkerchief which she wraps round my neck. The smell is sickening but complaining would not make her remove it. The sound of someone's unlatched gate bangs back and forth against its metallic post. It is a sound that ruffles and frightens me in ways I don't understand. The sound goes on and on like the implacable wind that causes it, and it is the wind I mind. I feel something is amiss.

Pink-ting, pink-ting, pink-ting. The sound makes me feel lost and helpless. On my lap is a big photograph album whose covers are made of heavy jacaranda wood with inlays of palm trees made from a lighter-colored wood I don't know the name of. I have been turning over the black pages of photographs neatly placed into white glued-in corners. I find myself looking at pictures of Arlette and me when we are younger to see if maybe we are in a hot windy place. I see us in Pouços de Calda where generous waterfalls fan white over dark boulders worn round. I see the water swirl round a white marble statue of two nude women, one of whose bottoms our black-bereted father is kissing. The photograph is filled with circles. Near-bye my mother sits with two women in hats and they all are laughing as if to say: "Oh, that Benny!" In another picture, I sit atop a white horse pulling a rough calèche; in another, Arlette and I flank our mother at the top of a hill. We three are frowning against the brilliance of the day and we all are wearing dark coats which makes me know we are up high somewhere. Only with height does one get cool in the tropics.

Arlette looks about five or six, I three or four. This last picture looks very European, as do we, like refugees from a bombed out place. It reminds me of pictures I have seen of families isolated from their men and houses by war, like the one that is going on in Europe, but from 1941, the approximate date of the photographs I'm looking at, to the end of the Second World War, the only separation we have from our father is the distance he has taken to step away from us to take the photos. Our parents are with Arlette and me all the time, so we take them for granted.

The things I know or think to ask about our parents are few. I know our mother was born in Santiago, Chile of French Roman Catholic parents, went to Oberlin College in the United States, came back to work for the National City Bank in Santiago. There she met and married our French father who was working for the Otis Elevator Company. Mummy's family is still in Chile, but we've never met them. I now know about my father's sisters and about his Tante Vette, but no relatives are in these pictures. "These are all friends from São Paulo days" Mummy tells me, and also points out Dr. Lane and Mrs. Lane and their daughter, Helen, whom my father admires.

"Do you see her? When she reads, she always has a dictionary next to her."

There are pictures of the snake farm in Butãnta, photos of our father playing golf, photos in a plane of Mr. Wilson, the father of my friend, Wendy. Nothing echoes wind or clanging metal. I tire of the pictures, put down the album, but that night, I dream I am suffocating in hot dry air that is blowing at me through expanding metal pipes that hiss and clang in an enclosed space.

With no need to knit for the soldiers anymore, Mummy is teaching me to sew for the foot-high, thin model dolls with movable joints like the ones artists position to learn how to draw.

Tante Gilberte has sent the dolls to Arlette and me—one for each of us—along with a whole wardrobe of knitted dresses, hats, sweaters and coats she fashioned. She and my mother are experts, but Mummy is also an inventive seamstress. The nuns have taught her at school. She sews tiny dresses for my doll and goads me to try on my own. I'm afraid of her criticism and, still troubled by the wind on the porch, I ask her to tell me a story.

"Once upon a time," she starts with my four favorite words, "there was a tailor who had a monkey he loved dearly, but this tailor was poor. He always was short of money to buy food for himself and for the monkey, who depended on him. Now the monkey loved the tailor, too, and he knew the tailor was sad. Also, the monkey was hungry, so one day when they had gone two days without so much as a mango, the monkey decided to help the tailor.

"He watched the tailor carefully, saw a bolt of golden cloth carefully put aside in a corner, and thought, 'The tailor will never notice I've taken that, so tonight when he is asleep, I'll cut it up into the breeches the Earl ordered.' The monkey had noticed how the tailor prepared the thread. 'He measures from his thumb to his elbow, threads it through the eye of the needle, doubles and knots the thread so it is now only half as long. He spends all his time threading and re-threading the needle, and his eyesight is so poor, he spends more time threading than sewing. I will take a long thread and I will sew up the breeches with one thread length before I run out.'

"That night, after preparing the monkey's bed, putting out some water for the animal to drink and taking a sip of water himself, the tailor curled up on a thin rug and went to sleep shivering. The monkey scurried to the corner where the rich golden cloth lay, took out the tailor's sharp scissors and cut what seemed like a fine pair of trousers that might fit him, for example. He then took a piece of thread the size of his whole body. With his quick fingers and good eyes, he had no trouble threading the needle, doubling and knotting the thread until he thought he had enough to sew up one side of the trouser legs and down the other. It wasn't long before the thread caught on the door handle near-by, the corner of the sewing table, the monkey's foot, and the cloth itself that lay on his lap. Pretty soon, the monkey didn't know where to put the needle. He had sewn himself into the cloth and could barely move. And this is how the tailor found the monkey the next morning when he woke up.

" 'Monkey, what have you done? Are you all right?'

" 'I wanted to help you sew so we could make more money to buy food with, but now I've ruined your bolt of cloth, my fingers are pricked and bleeding, and we are poorer than ever.'

" 'My dear monkey,' said the tailor. 'I appreciate your wish to help, but to know how to do anything properly, you need to have patience. *'Petit à petit, l'oiseau fait son nid.'*"

There is no need for Mummy to explain the story. I have heard her 'little by little, the bird makes his nest' before. Having patience is what I most need. I have lost my chances to play piano because I have not wanted to practice.

But Mummy is patient with me in times that are difficult for her. I frequently am sick with amoebic dysentery. There is medicine for it, but I fear the shots the pharmacist has to give me, and my parents, Arlette, the maids hate the fuss I make when he has to come over to give them to me. While I am sick, I worry a lot, dark thoughts about my health, my father's, my mother's. Doutor Martinho, a man who is shorter than I am by the time I am eight, tells my mother he thinks it would be good for me to have early morning walks on the Ipanema beach, a block away from our house.

Mummy hates the beach. She hates the heat—it already is too hot and airless for her by early morning—and she hates the sand. The sun that rises impossibly huge and red fascinates me, but the blinding light that reflects off the ocean hurts Mummy's light blue eyes. She is not feeling well, but no one seems to know why. She takes me for those walks anyway until I hear her voice lagging behind: "Denise, let's go home." Her tone makes it clear she can't stand it a second longer no matter how much fun she thinks I am having putting my feet in the restless waves. But I am not having fun. I know she hates this as much as I hate the shots, only now I hate myself, too, because I am making her miserable. We stop the early morning beach walks.

Perhaps she does not like to remember the morning we were in Leblon, a beach next to Ipanema, a little wilder, closer to the range of the Gavea's mountains, the Two Brothers. One moment she was standing barefoot in her dress of flowers watching waves tuck their spray into the sand near me. I waded in further. And then she seemed miles away, a speck on the beach waving for me to come back. I knew I had been caught in an undertow, knew she could not come after me. Lifeguards have rowboats near-bye to hurry out to people, buoys to throw out to them, but today, there had been no warning red flags on the beach and no lifeguards in sight. It was early and the beach was empty.

"If you are caught in an undertow and you cannot dive deep enough under the current, swim diagonally out of it," I heard our swimming teacher, Mr. Reyes, saying as if he were by Sally's, Arlette's and my side at our swimming lessons. I knew I had to join my mother and I knew I did not dare to dive further down into the water. How wide was the current? Suppose I surfaced right back into the middle of it where it would pull me out further and faster? I remember figuring out how I would start the crawl going back towards the beach of Ipanema towards our house, but I soon began to imagine what might be swimming below me in the water. I did not want to see jellyfish, a shark, or even any one of the big fish the fisherman dragged into Posto 6 at one end of Copacabana Beach to sell early in the morning. The fish were always big, had fins, and I feared sandpaper burns from their scales or skin when they flipped. "The backstroke is your strongest stroke, Denise," Mr. Reyes often told me, but even if I had not remembered his voice, I would have rolled over and started in fright. One-two-three, one-two-three, one-two three, one-two-three, right arm then left arm, while my feet were kicking one-two-three-four-five-six, one-two-three-four-five-six. I don't know how long it took me, but my mother had been able to cross the length of the beach to Ipanema by the time I counted my way out of the water. She held open a towel and wrapped me in it, both of us shivering.

CHAPTER TWENTY-ONE

Gaining Independence

January, 1946,

Querida familia,

President Truman has come to Rio. His simplicity is disarming, a straightforwardness, I suppose, that would make his reasoning to drop the atomic bomb have clarity—at least for himself.

Even months after the bombing, Movietone news continues to show us photographs of the mushroom cloud, the wind, height and magnitude making a zephyr of Vesuvius's explosion in 1944. I look and look and look again, and still cannot understand.

The Japanese reaction in Rio was as mute as their Emperor's when faced with the infernal reality of what happened. But then, their internment in this country does not make easy access to what they are thinking and feeling. And what did the Allies fighting in the Pacific think and feel?

How will the world look upon this act in one, ten, twenty years?

I send you some pictures of the girls in a flock of students with Truman on the grounds of the American Embassy. Denise has her arm stretched out over the heads of the other children (for once appreciating her height), and Arlette is beaming in the background.

I found a quote from Oppenheimer—not the more famous "I am become Death" he quoted from the Baghavad-Gita, but this one: "It is perfectly obvious that the whole world is going to hell. The only possible *chance that it might not is that we do not attempt to prevent it from doing so."*

Have we come to this? Tell me what you are thinking, all of you.

Love, incomprehension, and a fierce sense of protection, Queta

PS. To end on a more positive note: One of the practical results of the American appreciation that Brazil was the only country in South America to send an expeditionary force to Europe (the Brazilians were said to have fought so furiously and bravely at Monte Castello, the Italians thought they were crazy!) is the U.S.'s funding of a huge steel manufacturing plant called Volta Redonda, about which you may have been reading. Everyone is calling this venture Brazil's industrial coming of age.

* * *

In Rio I know it is time to go home when the heat is at its worst. Even the vultures, are not around. The walk from the American school to the *bonde* is a short block away. The bonde is a trolley that the Canadian Bond and Share Company sold bonds to pay for. Brazilians can't end a word with a consonant without adding the *e* sound, so bond became *bonde* and everyone uses the word, even the English speakers. I love the sound of the word, the *d* sounding like a *j*, almost as if I were saying in bad French **Bon Djeu**, but having it come out *Bon DJee* instead.

Since the end of the war, I have been able to go back and forth to school either with Arlette or on my own. I cover the distance of a mud-baked lot surrounded by a cement wall that has "Kilroy was here" written on it. The writing is accompanied by the cartoon of Kilroy's huge nose and the knuckles of his fingers on either side of the nose peering over the wall. I don't know who Kilroy is, but it is something else the Americans have brought with them, and I think it is friendly.

I like the travel to and from school more than I like school. It's not that I don't like school; it's that I don't pay attention. I get Ds in self-control and not much better in Portuguese where I don't have to day-dream because Mr. Geezie entertains us. He is tall and skinny and looks like a praying mantis. With bony knees at right angles, he chases Peggy Siefert up and down the aisles of the class as she runs away from him playing with her yo-yo. If this were math class, the teacher could use it to show right angles: Mr. Geezie's knees and Peggy's yo-yo. It happens every class. I admire Peggy. She and her sister have written the words and music of our school song:

"O, Escola Americana, we will always stand by you,
Sing your praises and be loyal to your colors, red and blue.
O, Escola Americana, sunny school of work and play,
You will never be forgotten though we wander far away."

If it isn't Peggy Mr. Geezie is mad at, it is Mario Dumont who's knee jiggles as fast as he is solving math problems. The teachers can't keep up with him. Mario is short and compact, his dark hair neatly oiled and parted so that it looks exactly the same every day. Or Mr. Geezie is mad at Demosthenes, who is very large and lazy, but he makes us all laugh, so we are on his side. The day I am called into the Principal's office and imagine I am being expelled for some reason, they tell me they want me to skip 5th grade.

I get As in most of the other subjects, especially in music. Mrs. Moore, the wife of the new principal, is short and blond and cute and she loves to teach us American songs. Mr. Moore is tall, dark-haired and elegant. We hear he became Principal when the old Principal ran off with the secretary and the money of the School. We don't ask about any of this because a) we wouldn't be told, and b) we don't care. Life with the Moores is wonderful, and Arlette likes their son, Larry, a lot. So do I. I know I could not choose a boyfriend of my own, but if Arlette likes one, he must be nice and my kind of boyfriend, too.

The American School is not supposed to be as good as the English School, but we like the mix of students at our school. My books at home, from *Les Malheures de Sophie*, to *Nancy Drew*, to even the awful one about *Strumpeter*, who has his fingers cut off—the picture shows him with his hands outstretched and his fingers dripping blood on the floor—are more interesting than what I'm reading at school. I look forward to getting home and head for the corner stop on the avenue streaked with trolley tracks.

Usually there is a man who sells sweets by the school stop at General Urquiza. His umbrella-covered stand holds a tray full of wafer cookies, sickly green, yellow, and pink candies like Turkish delight rolled in granular sugar. The flies land on all the pieces. Arlette and I know not to eat unwrapped foods. Why would anyone want to eat fly-specked candy? Might as well eat a cockroach since they've crawled over the pieces, too. Maybe that's why Brazilian cockroaches get so big.

There is a covered candy that I want, however, and treat myself to very occasionally. I can't think how I have the money for it since our parents do nothing to help us get ourselves into trouble when we are on our own. I must have left-over trolley money. The wrapping of the candy is black with small white lettering, and the candy is chocolate, shaped like a lipstick. It must be special chocolate or carob because it doesn't melt in the heat.

I can go home alone now and the trolley ride home offers the perfect time and place to pay attention to this candy. The trolleys are open and because of the heat everyone wants to stand on the running board and clutch onto a support pole. It's a place reserved for the young men, however, and I must plow my way through the outside curtain of male bodies to the inner wooden benches I share with a few other students, exhausted maids and mothers nursing and carrying children. The women sit. I stand. Arlette and I seldom come home together now. She spends time with her friends, the American, Martha Waddell; Irish Pat Sullivan, who loves horses, rides them well, has freckles and huge veins that stand out on her hands (I admire these features, want them, get them); the Swiss blond Amaryllis Mayerhoffer, as gracefully pretty as her floral name, or the Mexican Zaragosa twins, Rosita and Maria-Elena who live close to the school and whose house smells of delicious fried bananas.

I sniff the chocolate. I unwrap one end of the cylinder and start sucking at it. It is hard work, takes concentrated effort to build the end to a fine point which I can pretend is lipstick, then bite off to start to shape another lipstick again. It will take ten minutes of the trolley's stops-and-starts to travel from School to the Leblon Canal to get through the first quarter of the chocolate. I'll be starting to build fine point number two as the trolley swings 180 degrees round from Avenida Visconde de Albuquerque onto Avenida Ataulfo de Paiva. I'll be sucking and shaping the chocolate lipstick past a stationery store, the tiny hairdressing salon where our mother goes, a hardware store, a pharmacy, the movie house at the Ipanema Canal, a hub point for trolleys and buses to meet and for passengers to transfer. I can stay on the same trolley, but I haven't much time. Off with the chocolate's head and onto shape the third one. Two more stops and I'll have to push past the sweating black, white, and copper-colored men hanging onto the outside of the trolley. "*Faz favor. Com licença.* Please. With your permission." I scramble off, hop to the sidewalk. I walk past the skinny hole-in-the-wall shop our seamstress lives in, hope she will not be at our home where I will have to stand still on a chair for a fitting of another one of Sally's hand-me-downs that Arlette has already worn. Next comes the corner shoe store where I cast an envious eye at a pair of orange wedge-heeled pumps I'm dying to have because I think they look American. I run my hand along the rough exterior stucco of the buildings and turn the corner onto García d'Avila, one block from home.

The roof of my mouth and tongue are sore from sculpting the chocolate, but I'm nearly down to the last quarter. I bite off the third sharp point as I pass our dancing teacher's house and turn left onto Prudente de Moraes where we live one block from the sea. I aim my sandals at all the tiny round figs that have fallen on the sidewalk from the huge shade trees that line the street and crunch past gates and fences of the houses. You can't eat these figs, you only can step on them. Crunch, crunch and out pop the tiny hard black seeds. Lick, shape, bite, chocolate's gone.

I fill my quiet with songs. Along with the French and Portuguese ones I know, I am learning lots of American ones in second grade from Mrs. Moore. She teaches us "Zippity Doo-Dah" and makes us count 'one' between "It's the truth, it's atchall [one], everything is satisfatchall" so we don't come in too soon. I hear she likes to eat catsup on ice cream, but I think it is just a way for students to put together everything tasty about American food.

On my way home one day, I hear a *Pssst, menina*, a 'Hey, girl' attention request. I turn to see a skinny older man with a raincoat he has opened to show me he has dropped his pants to his ankles and his willy is hanging out looking purple and swollen like a banana fruit. It stands out against his grey skin and looks terrible and I feel sorry for him. I know I have to get away because this is not a proper way for him to act in public, but I know I can out-run him if he tries to catch me. He would have to cross the street first, and his pants would trip him. I turn my head back and walk quickly away.

Will I tell Mummy? The last time I told on the *pãodeiro*, who was pushing his bread wagon as usual along the street in front of our house, he disappeared. I felt it was my fault for telling Mummy that he invited me to come explore some buildings that were under construction. "No one else will be there to bother us," he had said. I continue home thinking about what to do.

I go quickly past the Beatties' home. They are American friends of our parents, but I am afraid of Dutch. She is small and compact, has lively shiny black eyes, wears her hair pulled back in a bun, and has a laugh that sounds of cigarettes. She is married to curly-haired Bill who is as short as Dutch, but whose eyes crinkle in kindness all the time. He's another American who works for the National City Bank. Maybe Mummy worked for him in Santiago. The Beatties were at Mummy's and Daddy's wedding. The Beatties have two children, Billie Jean, who is even older than Arlette, and Bud, who is handsome. Dutch is one of Mummy's friends who rolled bandages with her during the war. They encouraged us children to help.

I'm scared of Dutch because she challenges me. For some reason, I am helping her make the beds in her house one morning. Maybe it's one of the many times I'm recuperating from something and I'm not allowed to go back to school yet. Maybe Mummy is the one who is not well. Maybe it's the day Mummy is in São Paulo getting her gall bladder operated on. If I'm not home and not at school, it's certainly because Mummy needs to have me out from under foot.

"Do you know how to make a square corner?" Dutch asks.
"What?"
"Do you know how to make a square corner?"
"No."
Dutch shows me how. "Did you do that one right?"
"What?"
"Did you make that second square corner right?"
"What?"
"Are you listening?"
I do not ask 'what' again. I know I am being extremely impolite to say 'what' instead of saying "I beg your pardon," but I do not

wish to hear what Dutch may tell me. I am afraid that she may say that my mother is sick and that I shouldn't bother her, that I should leave her alone and in peace, that I should stop being selfish. I won't help Dutch make beds again.

CHAPTER TWENTY-TWO

The Figa

January, 1947

Queridos todos,

Brazil is booming after the war. It no longer needs to have an inferiority complex. They are selling their luscious coffee to anyone who wants it and can pay for it and, it seems, lots of countries can.

A fellow from Pennsylvania, Gilbert Huber, came to São Paulo last year to organize the Listas Telefónicas Brasileiras, S.A., what they call the "Yellow Pages," in English. He has produced three telephone directories—alphabetical, classified, and by street address. If this sounds banal, consider that up to now, we have had to look up phone numbers by looking under the person's first name. Imagine having to find our number under 'Benny!' Up to now, no company has known where to find new competitors or coordinators. It has been revolutionary. Newspapers call this a Brazilian miracle.

By next year, the directories will be handed out by hand to every business, governmental office, and residence, and the directories are making Mr. Huber a deservedly wealthy man. We all are thrilled!

Our girls are delighted in another respect. There is an American (yet again) called Kent Lutie who arrived from China to set up an ice cream company here. Up until now, we never had sufficient refrigeration and pasteurization processes to consider such a venture, but now he has come up with two ice creams the girls can choose from.

He called his company 'Kibom,' a variant spelling of 'Qui bom,' meaning 'How good.' If you want a chocolate tasting smooth ice cream on a stick, you ask for 'Chicabom' (Chi, qui bom!=Wow, how good!).I prefer 'Eskibom.' That derivation is not too hard to guess. A crisp dark chocolate cover hides vanilla ice cream inside. Even on a hot day, we can down the treat before it melts. Heaven! Are you jealous?

An unseen value to Lutie's enterprise is that he uses lots of eggs. It is the first time chicken farmers can count on a consistent market for their produce. The business community is flailing to keep up with new enterprises. Benny and his colleagues see nothing but possibilities and growth between the United States and Europe and Brazil.

It makes me laugh to think of the business letters I'd be typing at the First National City Bank: 'Dear Sir: Pursuant to our conversation concerning a loan towards the development of a fine chicken coop...'

I am hungry for your news, business or otherwise. Love, Q.

* * *

"Rub the figa for me." Our father tousles Arlette's blond curls, strokes my dark braids, bends to give us each a kiss on the cheek and saunters from the bright heat of the day into the cool gaming room that is the bar of the Rio Country Club. His moustache is nice and soft and he always smells good of fragrant soaps. The smell of tobacco doesn't hang about him because he smokes with a long white cigarette holder. The cigarette may never touch his hands or lips, but the smoke touches his lungs and, for the rest of his life, Arlette and I will see him have air-gasping bouts, hear him cough and cough and cough in the morning until his face turns purple and we ourselves stop breathing to keep him company until he inhales once again.

"Stop smoking," say his doctors.

"Smoking's not the problem. I use a *piteira*," our father says hanging onto the Brazilian word for a cigarette holder as if in

Portuguese, the *piteira* carries potent protection. In any case, it's too late. It's been too late for years. His lungs have been toying with his life since I am six, eight, twelve. All those little elastic balloons that blow up and down in the cartoons that tell us how our bodies work, how the lungs take in life-giving oxygen and expel useless carbon dioxide are in danger in his body.

Our family believes in luck, so we rub the figa charms that hang on chains around our necks, but we know Daddy has a figa of his own to summon. He carries it in his trouser pocket and will put it at hand on the green baize gaming table cover the way the other men do. When it is his time to take a turn, with his cards or dice at gin rummy or *bidú* or hearts or poker, he will rub the figa for good luck. He seems to have an inexhaustible supply of games he knows and, he is lucky.

The figa is an amulet shaped like a fist—always the left one—in which the thumb sticks out between the pointer and the middle fingers. I follow Daddy into the bar, finger his figa when he's got it out on the table, and rub my own on his behalf.

"Comes from Africa," Brazilian friends have told Arlette and me. "Used to be buried with the Nubian kings to give them power in the after-life (wink-wink, nudge-nudge). Just look at its shape. Why some places in the world, they'd think you had insulted them to wave the figa in their faces, never mind rub it! Came to Brazil with the slaves."

Well, the Brazilians are smarter, I think. They don't wait for good fortune in death; they use the figa for luck and joy in this life. Everyone has a figa. You can give one, but you can't ever buy one for yourself. If no one gives you a figa, you have to steal one. If the wood the fist is made of cracks, it means the figa has broken a bad run of luck and you have to throw the figa away because it has no more power left in it to give you good fortune. Figas come in household sizes and infant sizes. They have soapstone figas, and aquamarine figas, coral, amethyst, ivory and topaz figas. There are silver and gold figas. These last don't break so you don't know if they're protecting you or not. Babies get figas when they are born. Figas are good for everything and can never do harm. You can't wish for someone to have bad luck with a figa, for example. It just won't work.

The bartender is lining up beer—Brahma Chop—for the men. Every time a man orders a new beer, the bartender puts a thin round cork coaster under the glass. If you don't want people to see how many you've had, you have to hide the coasters in your pocket, but you have to show them all to the bar man at the end; you can't go home with the cork discs in your pocket in case someone finds them and asks "Whose are these?" They'll know.

It's not very exciting to watch men play cards and smoke and drink, so I go outside to where Mummy is sitting with her American, Brazilian and French friends. Many of the English like to stay in their own club. Mummy and her friends look alike in their flower-printed dresses, stockings, white pumps, their hair in *mise-en-plis*, folded rather than curled. A mise-en-plis and a manicure are minor luxuries. Most of the women have their hair done more often than Mummy, who is not very vain. Her nails look nice when they've been painted to leave a neat clear half-moon at the cuticle. Except for her engagement ring, she seldom wears jewelry.

Mummy is sitting at a table with Tante Chrisje, one of our many adopted aunts. I overhear Tante Chrisje almost crying. "I don't know what to do. I am so jealous of Charles," she is telling Mummy who answers: "Jealousy will only eat you up, not him," but they stop talking when I come up and ask if I can have a Coke.

"Of course not, Denise," Mummy says, but not unkindly.

"Orange Crush?"

"No."

I don't even like Orange Crush. It is smelly sweet and the orange die coats your tongue and lips, leaves a cloying after-taste. I don't like Coke either because it is too sweet, but our American friends at the Club can have them and, once in a while, Arlette and I would like to have one, too.

"They're expensive," Tante Chrisje says, pointing out the true objection. "How can you ask your mother such a thing? Are you spoiled children?" she asks. I know Tante Chrisje has been a nanny in her life and I'm glad she never was mine.

Arlette and I are not without gorgeous fruit drinks—mango, guava, passion fruit, papaya—but even these we cannot have at the Club. Everything, except our swimming lessons and my tennis lessons, is too expensive for children to spend money on and we aren't allowed to sign chits. Food and drink we get at home. Don't push your luck.

We would never rub the figa for anything so silly as an Orange Crush, but we'd rub it if Agenor or Raimunda or any grown-up friend played the *bicho*—the animal lottery—and if they asked us to wish them good luck. "Rub the figa for the monkey/the dog/the goat." You're not supposed to play the *bicho* because it is against the law, but everybody does it, especially the maids and the gardener and the cook. Raimunda probably doesn't bet. She's too Catholic and she knows she is not supposed to believe in betting or in anything but the church. She swallows the body and blood of Christ in church, but on many mornings, she first swallows the blood of the chicken she's killed, the way people who believe in Candomble, 'black magic,' do.

I think it is luck that sometimes Daddy invites me to walk along the golf course with him and Arlette because it smells so good of grass and is so full of color. The flamboyant trees have red-orange blossoms and the clusters of jacaranda are lavender when the trees are in bloom. The *quaresma* or lent tree has purple flowers, and the ipe can blossom white, yellow or blue. I love the scent of gardenia plants that are everywhere and I could stay in one place for a long time to watch the tiny monkeys called *micos* jump and prance in the shady fig trees. I have learned the bird song of the *bemtivi* (I see you! I see you!) singing over and over as if in time to Arlette's practicing stroke after stroke. Even the sky is full of color. Green and yellow parakeets flit through the tree tops, and red and green macaws perch on branches above our father's head to speak to us in a raucous cry as if their throats were sore. Huge butterflies flap their wings so that the sun turns their blue and purple colors shiny, and the blood birds—*pásaros de sangre*—flap in red and black. If we stop near hibiscus or some trumpet-shaped flower, we see humming birds the Brazilians call *beija flores* because they seem to kiss the flowers. There are snakes, of course, but they hide. If they don't, people call the gardener who comes with his fork-pronged stick to jam on either side of the snake's head to hold it down until he can kill it with a machete or, if it's not poisonous, pick it up to take away somewhere else. Lizards sometimes as large as four or five feet lurk about, but you don't have to go to the golf course to find them. We used to see them in Wendy Wilson's back yard, our friend who lives near the Itayangá Golf Club in Gavea, the sail mountain that is behind the mountain of the *Dois Irmãos* the Two Brothers, or the Two Tits, as our father calls them, which embarrasses me very much.

My favorite bird is the *urubú,* a vulture. I don't know why, exactly, but they are smart and I think they know about luck. They are everywhere—on the golf course, on the streets, around the playground of our school, which is where I see them. If we come early to school before the garbage men and sweepers have picked up orange rinds, banana peels, rodents, cats and dogs that have died or been discarded in the night, the *urubús* will be there picking the carcasses clean, yumming up the fruit pickings, scouring the ground of all the *lixo*, the refuse. The birds leave you alone and I think it is fun to walk through such a pack of them so close up. They stand about three feet tall, look and move awkwardly on the ground, but in the air, they are like all-black condors that fly forever and beautifully without a flap.

Urubús seem to know not to touch the *despachos* left on the street corners or by certain houses as if they sense these are collections of objects infused with unforeseeable powers—a smoked cigar butt, bird feathers, some chicken bones, a small glass of *caxaça*—a sugar cane alcohol – are set together, sometimes on a hanky. No person interferes with it, points to it, laughs at it, or says "Oh, look, there is a *despacho*." Better to walk past quickly, eyes averted, nose closed to whatever wafts of *maconha* the *macumbeiro* has smoked the night before to set the spell. Better just to carry on and . . . rub your figa.

In questions of health, the figa is all important. I know that I have to wash my hands when I come home, especially after going to market with Mummy or Raimunda, where we go to buy chickens, fish, colanders, wood clogs, salt, flowers, rice and beans, collard greens, these last three the staples of the daily Brazilian meal. The money we exchange with vendors is colorful when new, but most of the bills are so dirty and old, they look like thin fabric, ragged at the edges, the color of dirt with the smell of ages on them. "*Um centavo, por amor de Deus*," a penny for the love of God, the beggars ask. One hundred centavos make up one of those filthy bills, a cruzeiro, and it is impossible not to give something.

Beggars come in all forms: young children whose malformed arms and legs make you wonder what kind of accident befell them. "Their parents do that to them when they are small; that way, people will feel sorry for them, just like you, and give them money. You're wrong, you know," a lot of friends tell us. "You encourage their crimes." But how awful to be hungry, I think, and what on earth could they do without arms, or legs, or eyes? There are the plain poor, so skinny you know they are probably infested with worms and aren't kidding. There are the lepers whose blighted faces and hands touch the same bills you handed over for half a kilo of coffee. "Rub your figa that you never get leprosy," Mummy tells us, "but first, wash your hands."

I have to rub my figa because I am going back to the dentist's and I don't want to have any cavities. Most of the time, the American dentist has to drill my teeth so he can put silver fillings in. I hate the drilling. The noise terrifies me and the drill hurts my teeth, but today there is no drill. The dentist lets me play with a ball of mercury in my hand to distract me. I like to break the ball up into pieces and watch the smaller bits come together as if they are running into the center of my palm in a game to be together again as soon as possible.

"Oh, what a beautiful morning," I sing to myself on the bus ride home. I have left the dentist's office in the Esso building near the center of town in Botafogo. I have come alone because I am old enough, Arlette tells me. Mummy isn't feeling well, and Arlette's in school. I am going home and the day seems wonderful. The ride home will be beautiful because it always is, and the air smells fresh, and, this time, the figa has worked. I Don't Have Cavities. Maybe the dentist is making up for all the drilling he's been doing in Mummy's mouth recently. They think that the reason she has not been feeling well for so long is that she has some kind of infection in her teeth. They drill and drill, but they can't find anything wrong. Better rub the figa for her.

CHAPTER TWENTY-THREE

Safety

December, 1947

Queridos todos,

Here I am in São Paulo where our beloved surgeon, Jobe Lane, is taking care of us once again. This time it is not the girls with their tonsils (I have to laugh every time I think of their loving the toast they could eat after the operation better than even the new American ice cream); I am the one whose insides he is looking at. I was getting some enteric troubles not caused by amoebas, for once, and shooting pains in my back around the kidney level.

Doutor Martinho da Rocha, the darling pediatrician the girls have had since they were babies, was over here the other day looking into the girls' ears—inflamed from one of the many unknowns. I was in some distress at the time, so he asked me my symptoms. He made the provisional diagnosis of gall stones, so I have come to São Paulo to be with the only surgeon we trust. He and his wife are famous for letting his patients recuperate on their farm outside of the city. I can pat their horses there and have long talks with his wife, Kitty, and with their two fine children. Benny loves the girl, Helen. "She's always reading," he says with admiration, "and she carries a dictionary with her all the time." Our wild duo do no such thing but seem to remember every new word in whatever language is being served up.

They are doing well. Arlette has a lovely bunch of friends and has begun to attract the boys in school. She plays the piano, loves her English

Raleigh bike, beats Denise by leagues along the beach avenue. Denise insisted on our getting her a second-hand American bike with balloon tires, but they are so heavy, they make her go slow. If she is ruing her choice, she'll never say so. Denise skipped a grade and made the honor roll again after the first semester. How bored she must have been!

I hated to leave the girls, but they will be fine with Raimunda and Benny who will make a fuss over them at Christmas, and I want to feel well again.

* * *

"Where's Mummy?" are my first words.

I have taken the three blocks home from the trolley half running, half stopping to crunch the tiny hard figs that have fallen on the sidewalk. I needed to crush something. And it's hot and muggy, the kind of weather Mummy hates, and today I hate it, too. What if she's not home? I don't know when she left but one day she wasn't there. No one tells me anything in this house full of secrets. Arlette and my mother say: "Don't tell Denise. She takes things too seriously and she cries easily." I don't know what's wrong about taking things seriously. Arlette likes to be taken seriously, and Mummy wasn't feeling well. Did I remember hearing someone say Mummy had to have her gall bladder removed? If she is sick enough to go to São Paulo to be seen by Dr. Lane, isn't that serious? He is the only surgeon we know. His family is one of the ones who moved to São Paulo after the Civil War in the United States. Like us, he loves Brazil.

I have left the heat of the sidewalk and entered our cool high-ceilinged lobby but I still need to push open the glass and wrought iron doors that are heavy, take too much time. I'm in. I run up the broad marble steps that circle to the second floor where I ring the bell for someone to let me in.

Raimunda answers the bell. I love Raimunda. She is as black as I've seen anyone be, has a big bottom and a big bosom and very white teeth locked into gums as pink as the Double Bubble the sailors give us. I hug her like a buoy that has saved me from an ugly sea, and she hugs me back, but I do not have the hug that matters.

"Where's Mummy?" I repeat to this kindest of women.

"Is she home?"

"Come in, *meu bem*, my dear," she says unkinking herself from my tight arms. "Come sit down. I've prepared you your tea." Tea, for me, is a glass of filtered and boiled water and my favorite crunchy-crusted grey bread with butter and sugar on top. Raimunda is leading me towards the front porch which overlooks the street I have come in from, the place Arlette and I eat our snacks. If we spill sugar, the ants will come here instead of inside the house and we can hose them down. I don't want tea, and I don't want bread and I don't want further delay.

"Please tell me, Raimunda. Where's Mummy?" My nose is burning the way it does when I'm scared and about to cry.

Raimunda stops me before we reach the porch and sits me at a hard-backed chair in the living room next to the piano. This means I have my back to the rest of the house, the direction from which my mother would come if she were here. Raimunda is barefooted, as she always is inside the house, and she shifts from foot to foot. She does this when she is nervous, and I can hardly breathe. She is clearing her voice as if her own nervousness is closing her throat. I concentrate on her old toes.

"Sit here quietly, *meu bem*. I have a surprise for you." She backs away from my side and disappears behind me. I listen to her shuffle away on our wood floors, know she has crossed into the tiled area when I lose track of her sounds.

I sit with my gaze on the floor. If I don't move my eyes, maybe everything will be all right. Maybe Mummy had an operation and is fine now. Maybe my father brought her back from São Paulo. He was gone last night, wasn't he? And he was gone when he took her down, wasn't he? The moments tick by and I lift my head to look at the photo of our father with his arms around Arlette and me. The photo is on a ledge over the brown couch that forms a corner in our living room, the same couch that's in the picture. In the photograph, Daddy is laughing, as are we. I wonder why.

Raimunda would not have said she had a surprise for me unless it was Mummy, would she? How would I be able to say thank you for something else? Did I hear something? I listen so hard, I feel the insides of my ears will spill out. Should I get up? Go see? No, Raimunda has told me to sit still and I have never disobeyed her. I concentrate on the smell of the wax on the floor, floors kept clean and shiny by Argentão-even his name is shiny as in silver. He is a wiry thin Indian from the interior and has green eyes. He flirts with Raimunda whose teeth lose their moorings when she laughs and she clicks them back into her mouth. Where is Raimunda?

I hear shuffling, slow. Do I dare look behind me? Do I hear two voices? Are they mumbling? Someone's coming, for sure now. Why so slowly? And then Mummy is in sight and I don't know what to do with that sight. I jump up to hug her, cry with relief (yes, of course I am crying; let them be right) and hear Raimunda say: "Gently, gently, *meu bem*." Mummy would not have said that no matter how much I might hurt her, but I don't think I have hurt her, hugged her too hard. What is too hard?

"I'm so glad to see you!" I tell her. "Where have you been? What happened to you? I was so worried." I don't ask her where our father is or how she got home or how long she has been gone or listen to answers she might have given because none of this matters. And I haven't failed to tell her how her absence was a worry to me. Arlette would never be so selfish, but I am. Now, Mummy is here where I can touch and smell her, hear her voice and, of course, I will ask her to play piano for me, my favorite piece, the Chopin Goutte d'eau, because it sounds like a repeated water drop through the whole piece, and because she always plays it for me. Maybe not today, though. Mummy is so thin. And she looks pale. And she moves as if she hurts.

I don't remember where we stay after that, if she joins me in the living room, if she sits on the couch corner beneath the picture of our father, Arlette and me, if we go back to her bed where Arlette and I play with her jewelry box when we are sick. Mummy doesn't look as if she wants to play. As for me, all I can think of is how relieved I am. I will keep on rubbing my figa for her. Mummy is back. We all are safe.

CHAPTER TWENTY-FOUR

Leaving Guanabara

But, of course, our mother is not safe, and nor are we—not our father, nor my sister, nor myself. Our world, which was so civilized and plentiful in Brazil during the war, is cracking under an upheaval like the times that have destroyed our families in Europe, a world Arlette and I know nothing about. The war world Arlette and I have lived through has created in us no sense of danger or loss, no tangle of terrors to wrestle free from. World War II in Rio has been child's play.

With our mother's undiagnosed illness, Arlette and I are mobilized in a battle that is new to us. We begin to understand conditions of subterfuge that have existed in our lives and will recognize their increase, though never their resolution.

Our combat begins when we notice things change after our mother's return from her operation in São Paulo in 1948. She does not regain her strength. One day, when Arlette and I already are home from school, we hear voices shouting: *Madame!* and the inspired generic cry, *Nossa!* in the kitchen. *È a Dona Queta!* When we hear Raimunda identify our mother as the cause for alarm, we run to see what has happened.

Mummy has done some shopping and, unusually, decided to deliver the packages directly to Raimunda in the kitchen. For this, she chose the back entrance. She fell coming up the narrow spiral marble stairs leading to the kitchen and has cracked her upper arm bone on the edge of a riser. The bone is not sticking out, but you can see it in two pieces under the skin, displaced and breathtakingly painful. Why she was shopping in itself seems unusual as she has not regained her weight or strength since the operation, and her skin looks transparent.

Arlette and I stand by as shocked and ineffective as Raimunda who hops from one foot to the other wringing her hands and repeating: *Madame, Madame!*

When the telephone rings, Mummy asks her to answer but to tell whoever it is that she, Dona Queta, is not at home. From our mother's side, we watch and hear the dutiful Raimunda say into the phone: *A madame diz que ela não está na casa,* Madam says she is not at home.

Even with our mother's arm cast later in evidence, no amount of placating sooths the woman who calls so often asking our mother to get her out of the fixes she finds herself in with her staff. She wants help again, and this time, Mummy has not gone to her. Our rueful laughter comes later; in the meantime, somehow, we get our mother to a hospital where her fracture is set, but the pain never eases.

After her cast is removed, she cannot move her arm and shoulder without a wince or cry of distress. Arlette is her constant savior zipping her into and out of her dresses and fetching things Mummy asks her for. Perhaps our mother feels a stronger responsibility in training her older daughter, already a developed young woman, in the ways of caretaking. I still am excused, though I do not ask to be.

It is in this time period that Arlette takes me to a haircutter in Copacabana, far from home so no one might spot or stop us. Mummy can no longer braid my hair, but she cries when she sees me return in the unflattering crop. "Your braids, Denise!" she wails, not offering a bit of comfort. How has Arlette known where to take me? Has she consulted with Dutch Beattie, our most practical of friends who by then is also coming over to help our mother? I would not be surprised to hear Dutch say: "For heaven's sake, get rid of one more job for your mother. Cut Denise's hair!" I have been too spoiled to braid my own long thick hair, and no one has thought to teach me. I feel guilty and ready to know me in my new looks. I do not like them. My adjustments continue.

Our parents have two double beds that face each other through wide open French doors across the generous expanse of two rooms. How they share them is not known to me nor, at a very young eleven, am I curious about it. On the rare day that Mummy confines herself to bed, I notice Argentão has moved her bed (the bed we occupy when we are sick and playing with her jewelry box) away from the adjoining wall to our room to a perpendicular angle from normal. Her head is under the window and the shutters are drawn. Is it so we cannot hear her moan in pain?

Someone has recommended for Mummy an American doctor we've never used before. He has blond hair, pale sweaty skin, and blue eyes. He is mildly heavy, unpleasant, and enters the room without knocking. Without any preliminary introductions and inquiries, he shoos Arlette and me away from the door and proceeds to examine our mother. She is completely silent throughout. When the doctor opens the door, he is ready to leave and Arlette and I enter, hanging back a bit.

"By the way," he asks our mother from the threshold of the door, "how old are you?"

Mummy looks panicked. "I need a pencil and paper," she tells him.

"You can just tell me," he says.

"I prefer a paper and pencil," she insists.

I cannot understand why she is acting like that. Clearly, she can add, so as she hands the square bit of white paper on which she has scribbled something, I run forward and snatch it from her hands.

"52," it says, predicting the birthday she will have in four months.

I wait until Raimunda has let the doctor out. "You're not 52!" I say, clearly stunned over her advanced number of years.

Instead of denying or verifying the number, she bursts out crying, something I never have seen her do, and says: "He moved my breast by the nipple to listen to my heart." She is humiliated by this ruffian of a doctor, but devastated to know I am shocked by her age, and too sick to hold back her feelings. I sit by her side and tell her her age doesn't matter, but that I wonder why she felt she had to keep it a secret. We sit holding each other's hands in silence.

"Did you know how old Mummy is?" I ask Arlette later.

"Sure," she says, "it's on her passport."

I had noted 1897 on her passport, but the 18 before 97 made me disregard it. All the century numbers I was familiar with started with 19. Our father was born in 1900, Arlette in 1934, I in 1937. I did not bother to do the math. If I had, I also might have understood that she was three years older than our father, that when they married, he was 33, she 36, and that she had given birth to Arlette at age 37, to me the day after she turned 40.

Mummy does not seem able to get better. The doctors treat her for amoebic cysts, to no cure. The dentist looks for non-existent abscesses and pulls a healthy tooth. Another doctor has the wit to say: "Call Jobie Lane in São Paulo and ask him his advice." Dr. Lane suspects the gall bladder he removed was not benign. "Take her to the States," he orders.

His command and Mummy's illness become the generals in battle signaling when and how the family needs to act. Arlette and I are willing to obey any order that might help her, and our father's quiet is the continuum to our songs of hope that, like the war, all will be resolved.

At the end of 1948 almost exactly three years to the day from when our family sailed to the United States after the war, we sail again. This time, it is on the far better S.S. Uruguay, a regular Cunard passenger ship, but this time our father isn't with us.

"Otis won't let me go," our father tells Mummy. She is silent, but the next day I overhear a conversation that makes me stop on the way to the kitchen. Mummy is seated at her make-shift desk by our blue ones in the *copa*. She is calling the head of Otis.

"You can't treat Benny like a goat. He is not tethered to you and we need him," I hear her say into the phone to Mr. J. Had her brow not been wrinkled in fury, and had she not been cradling her arm in pain, I would have thought I had misheard her, but her cries for help are clear and go ungratified.

"You've gone to the States before, you can do this again," is the understood directive to us adolescents. I am four months short of my twelfth birthday, Arlette turned fifteen in September. We are to take our mother to the Strong Memorial Hospital in Rochester, New York when we arrive. There, our aunts we met in January of 1946 will welcome us into their homes again and make sure Mummy receives the care she needs. In the meantime, our Tia Mildred of Rio and Jundiaí days, now back in the United States, will meet us at the New York City dock and transfer us to the airplane to Rochester. We can do it.

Arlette and I pack next to nothing relying once again on relatives in Rochester to find winter clothing for us. "We can buy saddle shoes," Arlette says. What better sop?

We leave Raimunda standing on the sidewalk in front of our house wringing the apron she has on, unchecked tears and sobs broadcasting her dismay and fear for her beloved Dona Queta, and for us children. João drives us away in the wood-sided station wagon I am so fond of but, today, Raimunda's grief overwhelms all my other feelings. I need to see her again to take away some of her sadness, and I promise her we'll be back soon. She sees we are leaving everything behind, I think to myself, so she must know we'll come back home to Rio after Mummy is well.

I don't remember the specific farewells at the dock, only a flurry of hands waving, many of our mother's friends in tears. So many have already preceded us to the United States, but there are plenty left behind, many of them French. I know I don't want to leave, not my home, not Raimunda and Argentão, not the Dois Irmãos mountains going to Gavea, not the music, scents and tastes of Brazil, and not Guanabara Bay, which just a short time ago welcomed us back.

Our father quits work to meet us at the dock, to see us up the gangplank, and to settle us into our stateroom. Instead of being below the water line as we had been after the war on the Rio Jachal, we ride high in a room with a plushy bunk bed—I claim the top—and a separate single bed for our mother, pillows everywhere and the scent of clean linens. We have our own bathroom. Windows face forward and on the side, staircases up and down to other levels are near-by, and the dining room is close. At night we can hear the string quartets playing during dinner just like the string ensembles play at the tea room in the Copacabana Palace that Tante Chrisje takes us to.

Mummy, however, never sees our stateroom. Before we leave Rio, her skin turns a bright yellow-green like canaries, and when I kiss her, she tastes bitter of the bile salts her body no longer can get rid of. I don't know who decides to put her immediately into the ship's hospital, but that's where she goes, and Arlette is her constant companion.

"If you're going to come in to visit your mother, you mustn't cry," the nurse tells me, my lack of self-control damning me from staying close to the one person who could prevent my tears.

And so for hours, I run up and down the seeming hundreds of stairs in the front, mid-sections and back of the ship. I replace the possibility of thought by mindless action. I am shy to walk on deck where I want to be, but where I might bump into people who might ask me questions. I do not go into the dining room. A waiter, alerted somehow that there are two girls alone in a stateroom, but not appearing at dinner, begins to bring us trays of food. And then it is only one tray when Arlette decides to eat with Mummy.

"What do you talk about?" I ask her.

"I don't know," she answers, or "Nothing much."

Arlette has left a much bigger and closer circle of friends than I have, including boy friends and a special crush, and she is tending to our sick mother all day. I can imagine a tumult of anguish going through her brain, but we have learned well from our silent parents to keep things to ourselves. Our most intimate connection comes when she returns to sleep in the cabin and we play a "Guess what song I'm thinking of?" in which we take turns singing a song in our heads and transmitting it to the other. We rarely miss, and so we relive the carnival songs and American movie scores that filled our heads in Rio, and avoid confronting what is central to our feelings. The well-rehearsed burial of familial confidences controls us perfectly.

We do not celebrate crossing the Equator.

When we arrive in New York on January 6th, we do not have to wait for a doctor to board ship as we did after the war; instead, when the ship docks, Tia Mildred charms herself on board and finds us. The ship's doctor accompanies Mummy, who is on a litter, and the officials let us through. Her suitcase lies at her feet. Arlette and I carry our small ones with us.

"There's no plane to Rochester today," Tia Mildred says. "We're going back to the hotel you stayed at on Park Avenue the last time you were here."

This time, we will not be skating or exploring Woolworth's or going up and down escalators while Mummy shops. My memory does not record anything other than a red and gold patterned carpet that flows from the lobby to the hallways, the only sight my downcast eyes are willing to absorb until we get on the plane the next morning. I do hear Tia Mildred tell somebody:

"I called the house doctor to come see Queta to give her some pain medication but he was so shocked to see her, he forgot his bag and had to return for it."

I don't remember our mother crying out; all I think of is our flight to Rochester the next day. Tia Mildred brings Mummy a radio to take with her. It becomes her constant companion in the hospital, her connection to the outside world, a perfect gift.

We have never flown before, though our father took us often to the Santos Dumont airport to greet friends coming in from the last leg of South American stops. I loved to watch the airplanes land and turn, listen to the drop in pitch when the propellers feathered, feel the vibrations of the thrumming motors, watch for a familiar face as the ladders were brought to the opened doors of the plane. I am excited about flying.

We board the plane the next day. Mummy sleeps on the litter the hostess straps down securely at the back of the plane.

"I'll take care of her," she tells us.

Arlette and I sit in front and concentrate on the marrow-throbbing power of the motors. The propellers become invisible with the speed of rotation, followed by the miraculous take-off when we are pressed to the back of our seats and so, for a while, escape the bonds of gravity.

By January 9th, our mother is in the Strong Memorial Hospital. "We'll have to leave her alone for a while. The doctors have to find out what's wrong with her and then treat her," our aunts say, and start to ask us where we might want to go to school while we are living with them. Tante Dinah, the gypsy-like beauty who is full of fun says: "I'll take them to Harley with me" which is where she teaches French and Spanish, though she doesn't speak Spanish as well as Mummy. Arlette can go into her classes because she is in high school, but I have to fend in a lower grade with unknown teachers and unknown students who become a blur for me.

One day, Arlette and Tante Dinah come home roaring with laughter. They can't wait to tell me how Tante Dinah asked a student to describe what had happened to his neck, which was in a brace. *Je me suis fait mal au cou*, he was meant to say; instead, he said: *Je me suis fait mal au cul.* His neck became his ass. They laugh on and I join in knowing the mistake is funny, but I think how abashed the boy must have felt. And then I hear in my mind what I have heard so often from both Mummy and Arlette in Rio: "Don't be so serious!" I am not getting any less serious and, clearly, if I don't lighten up, no one is going to like me.

Friends of our aunts are kind to us, offer to have us come for sleep-overs. Our aunts always accept on our behalf, anxious, no doubt, to get us out of the house where we can't hear bad news if the hospital calls. They fear we will ask questions, but my habit of not asking a question whose answer I do not want to hear is so deeply carved in my head by then, they should have no fear. Arlette doesn't want to hear my worries either. She has no more way of coping with them than I have with hers, so we both continue to bury our thoughts and be silent. We don't sing telepathically to each other so much anymore at night because the invitation to guess what the other is thinking is unwelcome; instead, we give each other back rubs at night and argue over which one goes last so she can fall asleep with no duty ahead of her.

A bird-like friend of our aunts, Yvonne Gaudriot, lives across Highland Park, a spot we can walk to through the woods since the park abuts both her property at the top of the hill, and Tante Vette's mid-way up. Yvonne waits in her Nancy Drew-like roadster (though hers is black and Nancy's was blue), then drives us to visit our mother. When we get to the hospital, Yvonne finds a parking space as close to the hospital as possible. She noses in, pushes the car in front of her out of the way, then backs in to do the same to the car in back until she has injured all the bumpers sufficiently to move us in. *Voilà! Ça y est!* There we are, she cries in triumph and Arlette and I arrive in our mother's room with smiles on our faces and new stories about Yvonne. When we do not come with her, Mummy's first question is "How's Yvonne?"

January ices into a disagreeably cold and grey February. I count 4 different schools my aunts try out for me. I contribute little to my own welfare, sulk instead of socialize. The teachers recognize I am in class temporarily and do not gather extra energy to engage me. Arlette is happy at Harley, and she and Tante Dinah are sympathetic souls. They even paint together, Tante Dinah making watercolors that look like paintings of Matisse, Arlette finding latent talent to please all.

Our visits to the hospital are interrupted twice when our aunts say: "Your mother has to have a small operation." The operation is not specified but we are told the doctors will be giving our mother a medicine to make her sleep more often and more comfortably. Our visits are cut down.

I remember coming up to her floor once and seeing a priest leaving her room. When I walk in, I see her hide a Bible in the drawer next to her bed. She has never been religious in front of us and seems embarrassed to be caught with both the priest and the Bible. The next time we see her, she says, in anticipation of any questions she thinks we might put to her: "I like the visits from the priest. It's all right, you know." But I don't know. Religion and the dressed-up authorities who tend to it are something new, especially coming from a parent.

What I do know from stepping into church with Raimunda, and from the few sessions of Sunday school we attended is that religion is what people use for miracles. They ask the saints and Jesus Christ and his mother, Mary, to make miracles happen. It's like asking the *macumbeiro* to get rid of evil spirits, but Mummy had told me that you have to believe in these spirits to make them work for you. I will not ask about the priest and the Bible for fear it will show I don't know enough to believe in them either.

* * *

Around the 13th of March, our father finally arrived from Rio. Arlette and I had gone to see our mother that day. A resident met us outside her door.

"Your mother is very sick," he admonished us. "We had to remove an obstacle to clear an intestinal duct of some bilious poisons that were making her yellow."

I am shocked by this unusual short but detailed explanation of anything to do with our mother's illness; I understand 'remove' and 'poison.'

"You may go in, but do not disturb her," he said mid-way between trying to be kind, yet firm. "Arlette can go in first," were his next non-surprising words. Arlette does not stay long. When she comes out, she looks solemn but says nothing, and then it is my turn.

I walk into the room, take one look at our mother lying in bed, and am amazed by how well she looks. Her skin is white, not yellow, and her blue eyes have the intensity of blue I remembered. "Mummy," I cry. "You look so well but the doctor said you were so sick!" I fly into her with tears of consternation over how mean the doctor had been to tell us that. She is perfectly all right. Look at her! What was wrong with him?

The operation had made her better after all and my relief makes me notice other details—the stronger light in the sky; the radio lying within reach at her bedside table, a practical gift from Tia Mildred "to keep you in touch with the world"; a small bouquet of carnations on the windowsill, meager compared to the gaudy blooms Rio would have offered from our gardens; the washed out yellow of the walls; the rails on the bed like the white brass rails round our beds when Arlette and I been in hospital. Arlette and I got well. Mummy would, too. I weep in sobs.

"Don't cry," she says kindly with a sorrowful smile on her face and lets me recline against her for a short while. We both know everyone outside her door has heard me.

I emerge from the room to a barrage of furious voices—Arlette's, the nurse's, the resident's, all of them completely in love with our mother. I know they talk among themselves that I am complicated, emotional, impulsive and definitely not grown up yet.

"You weren't supposed to disturb her and you did! Did you think your selfish crying would not affect her?"

I leave feeling ashamed and wretched. It is the last time I ever see my mother.

CHAPTER TWENTY-FIVE

Dispersal, 1949

When our mother dies on March 17th, our father comes to us early in the morning. Arlette and I have been farmed out to a kind American family whom we hardly know, friends of Tante Dinah's from the Harley School. No one who is close to us, and who anticipated our mother's death, wants to be near us. We go where we are told.

Arlette is sleeping in one room, I in another. Our father comes into my room and lies down next to me outside the covers. He tells me he has just left Arlette, then says:

"Your mother has died."

He starts crying softly and I, the endless fountain of tears, have dry eyes then. "You can cry," I say to him then, not knowing what to say and not thinking to listen in case he wants to say something to me. I leave him alone in his grief. Does he think I am even more of a monster than usual?

Is this how he told Arlette? Did she ask him questions about how Mummy had died? Did she ask him if she had left any messages for her or for us? Did she give him time to do so? Did she console him? Is Arlette still in her bedroom? What's she doing? What is she thinking?

I go to sit in a sun room in one of the comfortable green-painted rattan chairs I almost can disappear into, hug my knees to my chest, keep still and try not to think, but the memory of the last time I saw Mummy torments me. I had given her no comfort. I am angry and ashamed of myself. I am angry when someone calls me for breakfast. I am angry I have to eat scrambled eggs and ketchup, the thick tomato syrup people in Rio said our music teacher, Mickey Moore, put on her ice cream. I cannot imagine it on either eggs or ice cream, and I don't want it now. I am angry I have to be polite to the people who are kind to us. I am angry at our father for having come so late to see Mummy. Why had he left her alone for so long? Could Otis really keep him back? I don't want to think about him or anyone or even myself. I don't want to think. I feel very sorry for Arlette who tried so hard to help our mother, but don't know how to say this. She will not want to hear it from me in any case.

When I go to breakfast, our father is gone. "Where's Daddy?" I ask our hostess whose eyes are swollen and whose nose is red.

"He's gone back to be with your aunts," she says.

"Why didn't we go back with him?" I ask.

It is not a kind question. Tante Vette's home has been our temporary cradle in Rochester since our first visit in 1946, but it has been clear the family hasn't wanted us present since our mother lay dying. Our hostess is the only one who has been generous enough to keep Arlette and me, and I notice that she, too, is upset. I feel sorry for her, and that she and her family are stuck with us.

She is standing at the door between the kitchen and the dining room where she had fed us. Her arms, empty of dishes, hang straight at her sides and the air around us thickens with our fear of her answer.

"He has things to do," she answers truthfully, without solace. She is quiet, dignified, does not try to hug us as she must know we would shrug her off, unable to accept her sympathy. She knows, as do we, that we need his company no matter how many things he has to do. My anger mounts. Arlette is as silent as our father.

What happens to Arlette and me through the next days until Mummy is buried is a mystery. We are neither invited nor expected to go to her burial at the Catholic cemetery, nor to any service in her memory. Do we go to school? If not, what do we do? Where do we go? Certainly we are not with our family of aunts and uncles. Everyone has disappeared except the people who have taken us in and, even at mealtimes, their children wander out of reach, keen to avoid the misery attached to Arlette and me.

"When are we going to see our father again?" I ask our hostess. "When is he coming back here?" I am careful to phrase my questions with time and place. I need specifics and would not dare ask if he is coming back, the same way I never dared ask if my mother were going to die.

Our hostess confirms that our father will be coming to visit us briefly right where we are staying. When he arrives, he speaks about his having to return to Rio and that he will have to leave us while he goes to arrange things there. He does not spell out what those things are and, habitually, we don't ask.

"The Grandgérards would like to have you stay with them, and so would the Munns," he says of two couples we knew in Rio who are now back in the United States, the former in New York City, the other in East Orange, New Jersey, a place we've never heard of, "but it would be difficult for them because they live in small apartments and they are too old." He doesn't question with whom Arlette and I might wish to stay. It is clear from his omission of our relatives that they are not considering sheltering us. I know they have been generous—we've loved our times with them—and that I can ask no favors, but still, why couldn't they keep us?

As an unspoken afterthought, we wonder if he has asked Yvonne Gaudriot who used to take us to the hospital in her car and park so badly she made us laugh? She has a huge house and her husband, Henri, is really nice and he seems to like us. And we could walk across Highland Park to Tante Vette's and Uncle Art's house and listen to their records and read their books and pat their awful long-haired fat cat, Floufie, but not have to stay around to smell the liver Tante Vette cooked for him. "Here, Floufie, eeg," she would call to him when it was ready. She had lived in Spain for many years before she married Uncle Art and she spoke Spanish. 'Eeg' was short for *higado*, the Spanish name for liver. And when our father was ready for us to return to Brazil, he would call, I think to myself in a rush. It shouldn't take long. At the end of five days, our father is gone.

Again we ask our hostess when next our father will return. She hesitates, but says:

"He will be back, but first he will have to arrange for many changes. He will have to find a new place to work and to get rid of your house."

WHAT? What does she mean a new place to work? In Rio? What about Otis? GET RID? WHY?

"Your mother made him promise that he would not take you back to Brazil to grow up there," says our hostess.

I do not want to believe her. How is it that Daddy never told us? How is it our hostess knows about this promise but we don't? If our aunts told her, were they sure they understood our mother's wishes? Had they been at her side to hear it? Who was at her side? The priest? Where was he now? What about Raimunda? I think, switching my attention back to Brazil as quickly as I can. I promised her we would be back, that we would bring back her adored Dona Queta. How can I write to her, tell her how much we love her, how much she means to us, how we hope she will be with a nice family to replace us? I would have made Daddy promise that he would take care of her, but now he is gone and he will never take us back home.

Not a cell in me accepts I won't see our mother again, that I will never hear her voice, those inspired 'yesses,' that I will never again feel her fingers playing a piano composition in the palm of my hand, feel the butterfly kisses she places on my cheeks at night, or the 'winky-winky' of her eyelashes fluttering over my forehead, or hear her sing *Los Pollitos*, a song I do not out-grow and will pass on to my children and grandchildren.

I cannot imagine that three years from now in Montreal, I will be going to school on a bus fogged over by the humid heat of human breath inside, sub-zero temperatures outside, when suddenly the scent of my mother's perfume hits me with such acuity that I push up and down the crowded aisles saying; "Excuse me, excuse me, please, I think I dropped my pencil around here somewhere," when what I actually am doing is sniffing people to find out which one carries that familiar scent she wore on her neck or wrists.

How will we tell our friends we are not coming back? How will we keep up with our friends in Rio and the ones who themselves have left? How will we find them? But, in truth, I am not focusing on any of these either. I am missing my father keenly and feeling both angry and sorry for him, too.

I think of something concrete to connect me to him, bring him back to us: if we can somehow get hold of him, might I ask our father to bring me the white patent leather purse I received for Christmas. It has a long thin strap, a zipper across the top, and the sides are in puffy small squares like some of the quilts I see on American beds. This purse had secret pockets where I could have kept just my own things. Might I ask him to bring the light green and lavender dress Sally handed down to Arlette and that was coming to me next? Would he know how to find them? How does anyone know our father will come back to the States in any case? He loves Brazil.

If we promised Raimunda we would return to Brazil, but didn't, why, I unfairly think in panic, should our father not break his promise to come back to us? And then I allow myself to think of all the countries and cities my parents had to leave in their lives: Paris, Bordeaux, Havana, Buenos Aires, Santiago, even the short times they spent in well-loved Chicago for my father, New York and Oberlin for my mother. I don't want to leave anywhere or anyone anymore.

"Are we going to be adopted?" I finally ask Arlette. "Will they separate us?" I dare ask, the thought of that separation being the ultimate despair.

"Of course not," are Arlette's music to my ears, and hers is the only voice I find safe and trusted.

And then I ask no more questions. I let my mind shut out anything painful, let it go blank, adopt the silence we use in our family during and after the war about anything important.

CHAPTER TWENTY-SIX

Revisions After Loss

It took a year, but our father did come back. He brought with him what he could bear to keep, the trunk we found only after he himself had died.

During that time, he took care that Arlette and I became legal wards of Don and Laverne Murray, the young couple who used to tease Daddy onto the tennis courts in Rio, the couple our father and mother had helped when they had had financial and personal problems, the couple whose *gasogenio* had burned up. Now that the Murrays were back in the United States in a cozy home in the tree-filled suburb of Maplewood, New Jersey, they could help him and honor our mother, whom they had loved. Our father's choice was Solomonic.

The Murrays shared our common languages and Brazilian tastes. 'Mamoushka' —as she named herself for us—fixed *feijoadas*, joined in our carnival songs, saw Arlette through a tonsillectomy (Dr. Lane's excision had not been complete), me through a false kidney infection. They delighted in the companionship we gave them and their son, three years younger than I, and they took us to the Jersey shore. We had the ocean again. Only thirty-two, Mamoushka loved to dance, sambaed with us in their living room to the records they had brought from Rio, and taught us the Charleston.

They filtered our father's *lembranças*—remembrances—mitigations for his emotional inability to communicate directly with us. They did not judge. They did not compare Arlette and me. They understood our *saudades*, the longing we had for our mother, for Raimunda, for our motherland, our home and friends, for the warm, messy profusion of nature, and for Portuguese, the language Arlette and I kept forever after for sharing secrets.

I had recurring dreams that I was back in Rio in our apartment, my nose leading me to the pungent savory-sweet scents of the cooking in our kitchen and in those of our friends'—tastes of rice and beans, fried bananas, coconut sweets. I fed my *saudades*, for the sugared stringence of guava and passion fruit, the sweet-salt odor of our waxed floors, the ocean, the stink bugs, the rains, and the bouquet of the cereus blossom outside our window one night a year. My dreams allowed me to satisfy my yearnings for the *batucada* rhythms, the carnival songs, our records, the crunch of stepping on dried leaves and figlets dropped from shading street trees, the murmur and music of the sweet people, the wonderful sound of the language, and I still heard my mother's voice, her songs, especially in the disjointed music and truncated lyrics as if in choosing medleys, she said: "Have a listen, taste; I do not know how long any song can last, or how much time we have to hear the whole thing . . . "

* * *

In May of 1950, as our school year with the Murrays was drawing to a close, Mamoushka said to us one day:

"Your father is going to remarry. He's bringing Lou here for you to meet today."

Mamoushka said this behind a plate of baloney sandwiches she knew we liked, a barrier to the explosive reaction she anticipated from us, and a softener to her news. "Lou?" Mamoushka even knew her name.

Once again, Arlette and I were the last to know about happenings within our most intimate family constellation. We had been four, now only three. Why hadn't our father told us first? He hadn't even told us he was back in the United States. Who was this woman? How and when had he met her? What kind of treason was this a scarce year since the death of our mother?

"I want you to behave," were Mamoushka's last words before the Murray's doorbell rang announcing the arrival of our father and Lou. The bell rang again, this time at the back door, the door we had used as a short cut to go to school and to escape to our friends' houses.

Our father kept to one side of Lou who stood framed by the doorway, the full spring foliage of tulip trees in the background. Her posture was straight and she held a purse clasped in both hands in front of her thighs. She might have been the same height and age as our mother, but there all similarities ended. She was dressed in a brown silk shantung suit and stood with her feet close together on brown suede peeky-toed platform shoes that laced round her ankle. Yes, of course, I would concentrate on the shoes. When had Arlette and I ever not noticed shoes and defined someone by footwear? These were Hollywood shoes that matched the color of her suit perfectly and there was an addition: an ankle bracelet in gold that caught the light of the sun shining through the leaves. The hat on her head was a large flat disc, larger and more stylish than a béret. It sat at an angle on her chestnut-colored jaw-length hair and matched her purse. Both hat and purse were black and full of tiny cylindrical silver sequins that also caught the light. She scintillated, but it was the bright red color of her toe and hand nail polish, and the matching red of her lipstick, swerving off lip line in the heat of the noontime sun, that held me captive and perhaps recalled the red lipstick and nail polish of the American woman on board ship in 1946 and of our shocking visit to her Park Avenue apartment.

Arlette and I did not wait to shake Lou's hand which she extended in a jangle of heavy gold bracelets. We turned our backs on her and fled up the stairs into our bedroom, onto the comfort of the white chenille bedspreads on the twin beds at opposite ends of the room, beds we had leaned out of to reach the radio at night to listen after hours to The Shadow and the Jack Benny shows. Whatever Lou signified, we did not want her, nor did we now want to leave the Murray's haven we had come to know and love.

Mamoushka galloped after us, closed the door, sat on Arlette's bed, and astounded us by laughing. "Girls, she is a surprise, all right, but I guarantee you, you will be happy to have her later on when you have your own families and she can look after your father." This was too much future to be able to imagine.

"Let me tell you what I know about her. Like your father, she was born in France of French parents. Their name was Bernard. Her own mother was hurt when she gave birth to Lou and had to be in a wheelchair. She died when Lou was ten. I'm not sure when Lou and her father moved to Brooklyn, but Lou's father remarried, to Lou's aunt, her mother's sister, so Lou knows about stepmothers. Lou was very close to her father, still is, and I think the stepmother turned out to be kind of mean. Lou left home as soon as she could and married a man, a jeweler, Charlie Moore, who was twenty-five years older than she was. He was very good to her, but she wanted to be independent and divorced him some time ago.

"Now, I'm not sure of this," Mamoushka continued, as if wanting to get as many explanations over with as fast as possible; after all, we would have to go downstairs to make amends and to greet our father, something we had not done at the door, "but I think your father met Lou between the time he was in New York and the time he was posted to Havana in the 1920s."

That meant before us. Before Mummy. He knew Lou longer than all of us!

Mamoushka dried our tears, somehow made us laugh, then hurried us out the bedroom door without giving us a chance to ask questions. She had deflated our shock and knew we had too much to process.

Arlette and I may never have learned properly what our father's and Lou's relationship had been either in the 1920s or through the years. Typically, we didn't ask, and nothing was proffered, and in the end, it didn't matter. Mamoushka proved right. Lou was steadfast to our father and they had fun together. Our father's judgment was sterling all along.

What we could not have imagined was what a fortuitous choice our father made for himself when he asked to transfer to Montreal in 1950. At that time, the Roman Catholic Church ran Quebec. It censored movies, books, and mores, but also ran the construction businesses that needed Otis elevators. The nuns and priests spoke 'proper' French, which was to say they didn't speak the Joual of the Quebecois which our father, who dreamt, sang and thought in French, had difficulty understanding. The entrepreneurs and business managers were fun-loving clergy who enjoyed fine food and fine wines, as did our father, and their business meetings took place over lunches in any number of the excellent restaurants in Montreal. The contracts kept coming in until Otis felt they needed to hand our father the management of their Maritime Province companies, as well as that of Quebec. Our father enjoyed traveling to Prince Edward Island, New Brunswick, Nova Scotia. He was professionally far more fulfilled than he had been in Brazil, and, now in his home office, he had his first language to indulge in.

After our first disastrous meeting with Lou, Arlette and I fished up the manners we knew were expected of us, and came to understand how hard it was for Lou to have two teenagers on her hands with only a very modest budget to manage. Our mother's illness had depleted whatever Brazilian *contos* our father had put aside, and so we made do with little, but enough.

Occasionally, Lou would disappear without giving us any notice. Of course, our father was mostly silent about it. When we woke the first time to find her gone, our father said: "She'll be back in a few days," but offered no further explanations. And so Arlette and I learned to cook.

We came to know that when Lou missed her father too much, she would fly to New York to spend some time with him in Brooklyn. Certainly, it gave her a rest from us. She would return with a dress for me, one for Arlette—never in all our teen years did we choose our own clothing, or have more than two uniforms for school. Arlette minded more than I, and for good reason. She dated. I recall Lou striking it right one time when she returned with a Kelly green coat for me and a pair of fur gloves the size of gorilla hands. Whatever I looked like, I was warm, and no one else had gloves like mine.

Lou made sure we got into the best English-speaking schools in the Westmount system which was outside Nôtre Dame de Grace, the district in which we lived. When it came time to go to college, there was no doubt she and our father would support us through McGill University.

My friends were many and golden through all those years, as were my teachers, a group of eccentrics who finally challenged me to think. And I finally learned how sex was negotiated by scrutinizing in the girls' room a comic book being passed around by my 8th grade classmates in which Popeye and Olive Oyl were doing it in full color.

When Arlette and I found our own lives, Lou was there to take good care of our father who continued to thrive in Montreal. Always a social being, he played cribbage at his club (piteira and cigarette still clutched between his teeth and, for all I knew, he still rubbed the figa), socialized with the English and French in different settings, reserved lunches with Lou at a fancy restaurant on Saturdays, and extended kindnesses to many, including our friend from Brazil days, Wendy Wilson. Her family, too, had moved back to the States after the war. For tumultuous reasons, Wendy was shipped off to a boarding school in Canada and was terribly lonely. Wendy wrote of him years later: *Think of what he did for me when I was an abandoned little girl in that terrible boarding school in Compton, Quebec. He took a long train ride on a grim winter day to visit me in the school infirmary. It was so kind.*

After our family's immigration to Canada, and my graduating from McGill, I displaced myself yet again to return to the United States.

Arlette and I ended up living our lives alternating between two cosmopolitan cities and on farms: hers were Montreal and Georgeville, Quebec, mine New York and Walton, in the western Catskills of New York State. In the city Arlette and I spread our roots laterally near the surface to come up for air and water in concrete cracks, our nourishment tidal with every new wash of cultures, tastes and languages we love. In the country, we sent down tap roots with the possibility we might not move so frequently again.

Arlette's taproot held more firmly than mine. My husband, Tom, and I continued to travel with our three children until we put foot on seven continents. Our accommodations were often in hammocks and tents. When Andrea was fourteen, Erika twelve, and Seth, seven, we finally took them to Brazil to introduce them to my geographic origins and to have a pioneering experience. A cowboy pilot wheelied the plane onto the tarmac of the high, red-earthed plateau of Brasilia, new to me, too. I felt the curvature of the world on that enormous expanse canopied with ever-changing clouds of white, purple and black during the day, and an over-salting of stars at night. The city was new, spanking white on russet mud roads barely paved, and with open markets selling sandals whose soles were made from long-lasting pieces of rubber tires cut to size and shape.

We continued to Rio, still beautiful enough to make me gulp my thanks I'd had the luck to be born and raised there. We bathed in the too-strong ocean, and gathered at corner fruit stands to drink up the guava, mango, papaya and passion fruit drinks that still had not been synthesized and bottled for export to the United States. We read signs that heretofore had been only oral history. *Lixo!* shouted Tom when we rounded a corner and read aloud a sign pasted onto a large garbage bin the familiar word I had not abandoned from childhood.

We went to the Amazon and rented a motored dugout and driver at the edge of the *lixo*-strewn market and river bank. We elbowed for space among the scavenging vultures and the ferry-riding passengers embarking with their goats, chickens, pots and pans bought at market. Armed with a pot of cooked rice and beans, but without life preservers, we put-putted midday into the main channel of the Amazon, where the pink dolphins were lolloping along beside us, and turned south up-river along the pewter-colored, silted Solimões. We ate the bony piranhas (in a welcomed reversal of prey), slept on the wood floor pillowed with bean bags in huts on stilts against the twenty-foot flood season of the Amazon. We exchanged the farmer's welcomed hospitality with anticipated kilos of sugar and rice, frisbees and ballpoint pens, plus some super-needed antibiotics for our first host's three year-old son who had a suppurating ear infection. In an act of unique charity, our host left us with a burning candle the first night when the five of us, plus the dugout owner, occupied their front room. Their family of six climbed together into the matrimonial bed in the only other room of their house.

Early the next hot and humid morning, we woke to a mist-scrimmed line of people standing on the high river bank. Word had traveled overnight that a doctor was visiting, and the river people had brought him their complaints. With me at Tom's elbow translating when needed, and our children checking in from playing soccer with the enclave's children, we witnessed a stoic bunch of farmers and fishermen, a few pregnant women with limps, missing fingers, skin lesions and other signs of hard-living in the tropics who had come to show the doctor something new that had befallen them. "What do I have, *doutor*?" "Can you do something?"

Our medical kit could not begin to cover what was needed for the mostly parasitic and septic inflammatory conditions. "Can you get to a medical center?" Tom asked. I thought of our impossibly remote Posto Seis in Rio, the beach-side clinic that tended to everything from burns and bug bites to hysteria, but there did not seem to be any villages nearby or large enough to organize these clinics. The people's heads nodded simultaneously in both yes and no, meaning a hopeful maybe. For reasons of transport, money and time, few would not be able to make the journey even to so close a city as Manaus.

Our return five days later to Manaus with our dugout navigator ("I know this river like the back of my hand,") began to seem like the tangling of the African Queen in the myriad islands that broke free to float in the rushing current of the river. My panic and resolve to get us out of there must have made some magnetic connection and, like a migrating bird, I got him to weave us out the way I directed. We extended our luck to go to the Coke-clear Rio Negro that lavished us with its different biodiversity. Eons of layered leaves in the water and their resulting tannins caused the slower river's black clarity. There were fewer bugs and, thus, fewer birds. We felt the river might do well with six fewer people, too, and headed back to Manaus and our exit from exploration.

Luck overbalanced my lack of judgment on this trip but allowed our children to have a sense of the daily routes and routines that attended my family in the lushness of Rio, as well as of the adventures and diseases Sally, Arlette and I had experienced in the wild of Jundiaí.

CHAPTER TWENTY-SEVEN

Lost and Found

Never having spoken to our father about any of his history, it took many years for me to understand the degree of my father's losses, the reasons why he might keep a closed book on the restrictions in his own life before, during and after his marriage, and of our times in Brazil.

I feel it was our mother's voice that kept him and all of us going through a conflagration of micro and macrocosms during the war. It must have seemed to him that with her disappearance we had reverted to a primordial chaos he had no means to shape.

The absence of dialogue, however, did not signify the loss of our mother's voice. As our exploding world cooled, we recalled her in French, Spanish, and Portuguese, depending on need or whim, but particularly in the English she promoted. We tasted it in our pastel de choclo as we amassed the grated corn, ground meat, onions and raisins she told us to mix; we heard it in her joy of the classical repertoire she taught us and in the medleys we came to sing together; we carried on her *cuidado!* that anticipated an incautious act on our part. We kept the careful quiet she instilled.

What was in her heart, however, remained a secret. Her dying wish exposed her wariness of our growing up in South America. Oberlin had branded her forever with its opportunities and encouragement of women's education, something she did not foresee for us in Brazil, and something she must have craved for herself. One more move on behalf of her daughters, especially if that move was to the United States, must not have seemed insurmountable or even aberrant. We would be three generations of transplants, that's all.

How did she view the news that arrived in redacted form from occupied Paris and Vichy-controlled Bordeaux? By the time she died in 1949, there were no doubts as to what Europe had done to its Jews, that the dragnet for them had extended to South America. Did she rue the silence she and our father had imposed to protect us from all war news? Did she wonder how we would react in time to this subterfuge?

As to the secret of our paternal Jewish heritage, the revelation our parents guarded against so successfully through the war, its verification came so late — Arlette and I were almost middle-aged — that it had about as much emotional significance as telling us we were part of the Milky Way, something grand and incomprehensible, too large to see wherein we fit. It wasn't that we hadn't suspected a possible connection as the years went on—after all, our maiden name was Benzacar, a Semitic name—but up until we left Brazil, we had grown up innocent of even the words Jew or Jewish. They carried neither definition nor import.

The knowledge of Jewish culture and traditions began piling up once we moved to Montreal. It came through the simple processes of going to school with and living among many self-identified Jewish friends; of noting when they were not in school because of specific religious holidays uncelebrated by the rest of us; of being properly excluded from Sweet Sixteen parties at Ruby Foo's on Decarie Boulevard; of understanding they had special cuisines from the Kosher smoked meat sandwiches dripping tasty fat to the ascetic taste of matzoh. My education of the Jewish experience expanded through immersing myself in books about a Second World War in Europe that I had known nothing about as a child in Brazil. Elie Wiesel's *Night* and William Shirer's *The Rise* and *Fall of the Third Reich* introduced me to the organized obscenity of the Holocaust.

When in his twenties—and tired of not knowing his genealogy— our son, Seth, went to the mayoralty in Bordeaux during the year he was exchanging construction skills for French lessons in Le Chambon, Cevenol, coincidentally itself a haven for Jewish children during the war.

"Here's your family history," he had said upon his return. Written in his meticulous and cramped writing, he dropped onto the kitchen table a folder he had copied from the files of births and deaths.

There he was, our father's father, Joseph Benzacar, listed in a long line of alternating Moseses and Josephs dating back to the 1500s, Sephardic Jews who had moved from Morocco to Portugal to settle finally in Bordeaux in the late 1700s.

Specifics petered out in the 1940s, so I started my own research through different Jewish agencies. During a visit to the Holocaust Memorial Museum in Washington , D.C., I consulted with one of the excellent librarians on staff. He pulled from their extensive files an alphabetical list of those Jews who had been carted off to any one of the many concentration and extermination camps during the war, and there I found Joseph Benzacar.

Epilogue

In November 2011, Tom and I travelled to Bordeaux in search of family history. I stopped a stranger to ask directions to the Archives clearly marked on the map, but invisible from view.

"The Archives have moved," he said amiably, "but go look at the old building anyway. Oh, it's a Monday. The Archives are closed in any case." He gave the very French shrug that says "What can you do about it?" then asked what I was in search of.

"I think there has been a street named after your grandfather," he said with some excitement when I gave my grandfather's name. " I have written a great deal about Bordeaux. Joseph Benzacar is a respected name. Mine is Plane, by the way, easy to remember because it's in every airport," he said extending a beautifully manicured hand from which he had first pocketed into his camel's hair coat a set of BMW keys.

I emailed our family about the encounter, and upon returning home, learned our granddaughter, Téa, had searched the internet for a possible Joseph Benzacar street or avenue. There was, indeed, a street, Le Professeur Benzacar but, in addition, she found via YouTube a ceremony that had taken place in the 7th arrondissement of Bordeaux on May 6, 2008 in which Alain Rousset, the Regional Counsellor of Aquitaine—the region in which Bordeaux is found—was expunging from a Square the name of a Vichy collaborator by the name of Poplawski (the very same University colleague Joseph imagined would not denounce him), and renaming it Square Joseph Benzacar.

"It is time we redressed some of the crimes from that dark time," said M. Rousset.

As part of the dedication ceremony, Brigitte Nabet, then Counsellor of the Municipal Socialist Party in Bordeaux, read aloud from a letter my grandfather had written to the Mayor on the 21st of October, 1940, concerning the Vichy Statute of the Jews.

Monsieur le Maire,

En exécution du Statut des Juifs en date du 18 octobre, j'ai été déchu sans sursis du mandat de Conseiller Municipal et, dans un délai de deux mois, du titre honorifique de membre du Corps enseignant.

Né à Bordeaux en 1862, étudiant, Avocat à la Cour, Professeur de la Faculté de Droit de Bordeaux pendant plus de 35 ans, Adjoint au Maire de Bordeaux pendant plus de quinze années, je suis désormais classé parmi les citoyens à capacité réduite.

Vainement mon bisaïeul aura fixé son domicile à Bordeaux en 1781, tous ses enfants et descendants, dont mon grand-père, mon père, seront nés à Bordeaux en 1789, en 1826, seront décédés dans cette Ville, je suis devenu à 78 ans un Français de qualité inférieure. Au surplus, je ne réclame point l'octroi d'un relèvement d'incapacité prévu par l'article 8 du Statut. Je n'ai point rendu à l'Etat Français des services exceptionnels. Je me suis exclusivement efforcé de remplir mon devoir dans toutes les branches de mon activité.

Mes étudiants, mes condisciples, mes confrères, mes collègues, m'ont constamment témoigné leur estime, leur sympathie. Aujourd'hui, mon rôle social est achevé.

L'ancien Doyen du Conseil Municipal doit remplir un dernier acte : exprimer à tous les regrets de la rupture imprévisible d'une longue collaboration amicale.

Veuillez agréer, Monsieur le Maire, l'assurance de mes sentiments affectueusement respectueux
   signé: BENZACAR

Bordeaux, October 21, 1940

Mr. Mayor,

By the enforcement of the Statute of Jews dated October 18th, I was summarily stripped, without reprieve, of my commission as Municipal Counsellor and, with a two month allowance, of the honored title of member of the Teaching Faculty.

Born in Bordeaux in 1862, student, lawyer at Court, Professor in the Faculty of Law of Bordeaux for thirty-five years, Deputy Mayor of Bordeaux for more than fifteen years, I am henceforth classified among the citizens of restricted capacity.

In vain, my great-grandfather made his home in Bordeaux in 1781, all his children and descendants, among them my grandfather, born in Bordeaux in 1789, (and) my father in 1826, will die in this City; (yet) I have become at 78 years of age a Frenchman of inferior quality. Beyond that, I do not accede to the statement of incompetence provided by article 8 of the Statute. I have not given any exceptional services to the French State (but) I have made every effort to fulfill my duty exclusively in all branches of my activity.

My students, my fellow schoolmates, my friends, my colleagues have constantly shown me their esteem and sympathy. Today, my role in society has ended. The former Dean of the Municipal Council must carry out a last act: to express to all the sorrow of the unforeseen rupture of a long (and) friendly collaboration.

Please accept, Mr. Mayor, my sincere and respectful affection,
   signed: Benzacar

I was overwhelmed by the elegant concision of his accomplishments, and simplicity of his outrage. I wondered if the original letter were extant. How nice it would be to see my grandfather's script, a style that often carries in families the way the shape of teeth do, the way family members walk, or the sounds of voices and laughter. All but his writing had been obliterated.

With the help of the internet, I found Brigitte Nabet's web page, wrote to thank her for reading aloud this first encounter with my grandfather's mind and emotions, and asked about the original copy of the letter.

Her answer was immediate. With no word about the original letter, she instead wrote, "Your cousin in Paris, Nicole Rodrigues-Ely, has been asking about any members of Joseph's family. Up to now, no one has turned up, yet here you are. I have forwarded her your email."

My cousin? The only cousin I knew about in Paris was Alain Ferry, a half-cousin I knew and liked well, but completely unrelated to my grandfather. Now here was Nicole, granddaughter of Joseph's brother, Nathaniel. That made Nicole, Arlette and me direct cousins removed by two generations.

Pas vrai! Were Nicole's first words in an email to me. *Not true! I knew Joseph. He and my grandfather lived in Bordeaux with their respective families. I didn't know Joseph had been married before, nor that the marriage had produced any children.*

In March of 2013, less than fifteen months after Brigitte put us in touch with one another, I flew to Paris. Nicole and I met at her apartment on the Avenue de la Grande Armée, a stone's throw from the Arc de Triomphe, and with a direct view of the Eiffel Tower. My gaze, however, was only on her as the door to the tiny elevator cage I was riding in opened to reveal Nicole standing at her much larger apartment portal.

The great irony is that she looked more like my mother than my father. Under 5 feet tall, with white curly hair and the bluest eyes

I'd ever seen, she radiated a joy that bounded into the hall before we even hugged. The laugh was strictly Benzacar, deep-throated, delightful. And what a funny sight I must have been to her—over 5'9" with winter boots on—and a mop of greying hair. Only my eyes of a duller blue hinted we might be related. I had to bend to hug her, and she had to strain her neck to embrace me. It was impossible to uncrease our smiles or to know where to start. Nicole made it easy by cracking a bottle of champagne and offering a pyramid of dark chocolates. *C'est normale!*

I soon learned that her 'normale' was set at a very high level. In her mid-eighties, she ran circles intellectually, culturally and humorfully around most giants I had encountered.

Her apartment was filled with leather-bound books, tapestries, paintings, watercolors and memorabilia returned to her from her parent's and grandparent's homes after the war. Remarkable among several articles displayed in a glass-fronted cabinet was the yellow cloth star she had been made to sew onto her coat during her peripatetic early life in France, when she and her widowed father were keeping one step ahead of the Nazi dragnet. Her father ultimately was able to leave her to end her school years in Biarritz in a section protected by the Americans. Beyond these revelations, Nicole was unwilling to speak.

One room of her apartment was devoted to seeing patients in her practice as a psychiatrist and psychoanalyst, but she skillfully skirted any talk of her professional status either.

Unmarried, Nicole had devoted her life to discovering and keeping alive the genealogy of our families, and to researching what the matters of daily life must have felt like for her grandparents under Vichy control. She showed me a family tree she had hand-written in a small, European script I found puzzling to decode at first, but came to learn with practice. Missing, however, were any entries following her great uncle, Joseph's, name.

Didn't you tell me you travelled to Israel a few years ago? she asked.

"That's right. 2008."

Did you go to Yad Vashem? she asked of the museum of the Shoah in Jerusalem.

"I did."

Did you think to research your grandfather's name?

"I always do at any Holocaust site or museum."

Well, did you not notice my name as the one who had recorded his into their library of those annihilated in the death camps?

"I did, as a matter of fact, and even asked the librarian about it. I told her I did not recognize the name Rodrigues-Ely as being a family name."

"Not to worry," the librarian had said. "The important thing is that your grandfather is recorded in our files. Often it is a complete stranger who has come upon a source of victims and makes sure to enroll them for posterity. Perhaps that is your case."

You didn't think to ask for an address? A possible relationship? Nicole asked in disbelief.

"It never crossed my mind," I had to admit, like the genealogical dilettante she convinced herself I was. "I had no idea Joseph had a brother. I only knew he had three children with my non-Jewish grandmother, Marguerite: Dinah, Jean (our father, "Benny") and Gilberte. When Marguerite divorced him, Joseph, according to Napoleonic law, kept the children."

What became of Marguerite? Nicole wanted to know.

"She moved back to Paris, re-married another professor she had met in Bordeaux, and had their daughter, Jacqueline, Alain's mother."

I spent three days telling Nicole much of what the reader has discovered in these pages; in addition, Nicole was curious to come to grips with Arlette's and my Chilean-French side of the family. It was a lot to absorb but, with her spirit of inquiry, curiosity and enthusiasm, she would discover its mysteries. What we both shared was the loss of our parental grandparents in Auschwitz; together, we would save whom we could.

When I asked her if she had any personal details about Joseph—did he smoke? like cats? draw? what was his voice like? how was it he became so involved in architectural planning of Bordeaux? whence my father's talent in drawing and in architectural details? and would she be willing to detail for me her own considerable escapes as a child in France during the war? Via email she gave succinct and to-be-respected answers.

Je n'ai aucun souvenir spécial de ton grand'père que j'aimais rencontrer car il me donnait l'impression d'aimer les enfants. Désolée de ne pouvoir t'en dire plus. Ton père t'en avait raconté d'avantage et je garde en souriant sa façon de chanter la Marseillaise . . . Je regrette de ne pas avoir connu ton père.

Je n'ai aucune envie de raconter quoique ce soit me concernant; je trouve en avoir trop dit: cela est du passé; comme tout le monde il faut faire avec et se dire que tout aurait pu être pire (cette expression française m'exaspère car elle laisse à penser que l'on regrette qu'elle n'ait pas été pire; en anglais « may » et « must » sont plus précis). Reparler de la guerre? à quoi bon? Je n'ai pas subi le sort de nos grands-parents, alors: rien à dire. Chacun son sort; je ne trouve pas que tu aies eu une vie si gaie à partir de la disparition de ta mère . . . Bref.

I have no special memories of your grandfather whom I enjoyed meeting as he gave the impression he liked children. Sorry not to be able to offer you more. Your father gave you enough and I keep smiling when I recall his way of singing the "Marseillaise" [to cover up for his young sisters when they had to pee while crossing a park. 'That way, people will pay attention to me and not to you!']. *I regret not having known your father.*

I have no wish to speak of myself about any matter. I feel I said too much; all that belongs in the past. As with everyone, one deals with what one is given and tells oneself that it could have been worse (that French expression drives me crazy as it implies that one regrets that things weren't worse. In English "may" and "must" are more precise.) Speak of the war? To what purpose? I did not fall prey to the end our grandparents did; therefore, nothing to say. Everyone has his own fate. I am under the impression that life for you was not so happy after your mother died. Enough.

We parted after too little time together but filled the subsequent void with a flurry of correspondence. Learning through my senses, as I do, I knew I needed to ground myself in the soil of my grandfather to incorporate the plentiful and meticulously noted genealogical information Nicole had amassed through the years. I returned to see her in late November of 2014 when events colluded to bring us to Bordeaux together.

In January of that year, Paris had mounted an exhibit to commemorate the seventieth anniversary of the roundup of Jews from the Great Synagogue on the Avenue du Grand Rabin Joseph Cohen in Bordeaux. The Vichy government had ordered Jewish families to congregate there—with their valuables, of course. Those who were not slaughtered in situ were stripped of their possessions and taken away for the ultimate solution to their despised existence.

The Nazis pillaged the Synagogue, left it as bare as if locusts had devoured the countryside (but, like the locusts, also ignored the living roots). There were stories of a few miraculous escapes on the part of young people (a boy of seven, who was able to climb the rafters of a bathroom and remain undetected when the Nazi soldiers broke in looking for anyone in hiding) and of the very few non-Jewish citizens who would hide them.

It was in repudiation of that unforgivable era that Nicole, especially invited for her enormous contributions to the history of the Benzacar patriarchs, and I travelled to Bordeaux.

At the time of our visit, Bordeaux had named after Joseph Benzacar not only a Street and a Place, but one amphitheatre in the recently renamed Montesquieu-Bordeaux IV University's School of Law, and another at a second campus in the City.

Too late, said Nicole thinking of her grandfather, too, who had passed into lesser public recognition.

"Might it be better late than never?" I asked, but Nicole was not assuaged. What mattered was a life, not commemorative plaques to counter years of culpability and guilt.

Bordeaux's pores breathed and sweated its years of collaboration. Imbedded in the paving stones on the sidewalk outside the station was a long brass rectangle. Inscribed thereon were the names of those sent to the holding camps by railway cars that stopped in a semi-hidden side of the St. Jean Station. Symbolically and actually, one still might step on the deportees.

We took a taxi to the Jewish cemetery off the Cours de Marne in the old Jewish Quarter of low, small houses. It was here that we found the Rue Professeur Benzacar, but not before Nicole had the taxi driver stop before a high-walled enclosure with a small door, and asked him to wait. She rang a bell for admittance and the cemetery attendant let us into a charmingly green enclosure whose tombstones were variously covered in moss, lichen or ivy. Some of the tombstones bore remarkably non-Hebraic alphabets and symbols (a heart, palm trees, a Zodiac-like sign) in testament to the mixture of religious expressions from the early days of the Marranos settlements in Bordeaux, Jews who had converted to Roman Catholicism to escape execution at the hands of the Spanish Inquisition in the late 15th century, but who covertly kept their Judaism to practice once out of Spain. The pitched shape of the cover stones reminded me of Ottoman era tombs I had seen in southern Turkey. It pleased me to see such organic markers of other diaspora. No one had been buried here since the late 1800s.

Now you will see where your ancestors are buried.

We drove to a second cemetery where Nicole had been giving money to maintain the tombs of our common ancestors, but she had a special project in mind.

With the attendant in tow, Nicole led me to the two massive stones that stood side by side where our great-grandparents, Amélie and Henri Benzacar, were buried, parents of their two murdered sons, our grandfathers.

As additional testament to the continuity of our paternal heritage, Nicole arranged with the keeper of the tombs to add the names of their sons to the base of the heavy stone slabs that covered their tombs. One inscription gave the name and date of birth of their son, Nathaniel Aaron, Nicole's grandfather. Alongside his were Nathaniel's wife, Emma Rebecca, with the words "Mort Pour la France, 1944." Two names remained to testify that Henri and Amélie had had another son, Joseph, and that he and his wife, Juliette, similarly had died for France.

The still-waiting taxi drove us into the beautifully renovated and cleaned center of Bordeaux where our hotel was in walking distance to the University, the Mayoralty, the exhibition hall, and the respective homes Nathaniel and Joseph had lived in.

Nicole and I entered the Faculty of Law building and faced a wide white marble staircase that separated into two graceful flanks leading further upwards. We held onto the filigreed railings to the landing where on one side, a commemorative plaque read:

**In Memory
of Joseph Benzacar
1862-1944
Professor of Political Economics
Died in Deportation
And of the students
Who died for France
1939-1945**

Twenty-one names followed.

A guard let us into the freshly renovated lecture hall named in my grandfather's honor. It was an antiseptic space, beautifully lit, but with no crochets for me to hook onto in a personal way. Certainly, Bordeaux was bending over backwards to make up to a man who devoted his life to it, but whom the citizens of that time miserably betrayed.

We met with M. Marc Malherbe, Head of the Conference who had written a publication, *Figures d'Aquitaine: de la célébrité à l'oubli*, published by the University Presses of Bordeaux. In it he had devoted a chapter to Joseph Benzacar, his predecessor in the Montesquieu-Bordeaux IV Faculty of Law. In addition, through a valued friend of his and old-book collector, Jean-Pierre Duprat, he sent me two compilations of my grandfather's writings (and, yes! with samples of his clear script). They ranged from legalities of Roman contract law from the first to the sixth centuries of the Empire, to the more contemporary legalities of French contract law on manual accidents at work. Researching in English, but writing in French, Joseph dissected the distribution of capital in American industries, and in British Fair Trade. Perhaps his most quoted paper in lecture halls had to do with the drought that destroyed the different wheat and grains in the late eighteenth century, led to starvation among the masses, and figured as the tipping point of the French Revolution. His writing was clear, enlightening, and unaffected.

Nicole had been in close contact with M. Malherbe to consult on Joseph's personal history for *Figures d'Aquitaine: de la célébrité à l'oubli*, and the two of them became my mainstays in revealing the extent of Joseph's professional career as an author, jurist, economist, lawyer, professor and, lastly, adjunct mayor of Bordeaux. Politically, this polymath was considered a radical Socialist. In 1931, he was bestowed the Chevalier de la Légion d'honneur, yet in 1940, the Germans changed that *honneur* to *honir*—shame. The Vichy French supported that disgrace. It was time for truth and reconciliation.

Nicole and I joined M. Malherbe; the Mayor; Alain Juppé (former Prime Minister of France); Dr. Aouizérate, President of the Israeli Consistory of Bordeaux and organizer of the exposition; the multiple representatives of the City Councils; attendees, and the media to wander through the hallways where the exhibit was on display. It consisted of carefully documented and mounted black and white photographs of members of Bordeaux's Jewish community, who had been deported and murdered during the war. The extensive displays included a comprehensive series of letters from which survivors and descendants identified their progenitors, siblings, and extended relatives. From there, we moved to a spacious and elegantly appointed *grande salle* adjoining the handsome gardens my grandfather's office faced, and from which Nicole, as a young child, enjoyed watching her great-uncle perform marriage ceremonies.

Nicole had proposed beforehand to M. Malherbe that I, a newly discovered direct descendant of Joseph Benzacar, speak in honor of my grandfather who was being singled out among the many former worthy citizens. *Certainly she speaks French!* Nicole assured him, omitting my obvious traces of foreign accents and lack of practice. And so, I was added to the roster of speakers.

As a French-Brazilian-American citizen who had lived out the war years in the beauty, splendor, safety and generosity of Brazil and Brazilians, I felt a fraud. In terms of religious background, mine was secular and pantheistic at the same time. I prized the Golden Rule, a moral code common to many philosophies, but I had no educated basis or wish to adopt the theology, history, beliefs and practices of my grandfather, whose ancient religion bound the others present at the ceremony. Until the immediate past, I had lived in ignorance of Joseph, and had had no inkling of what he had contributed in his life, or suffered in his death.

I followed the aforementioned dignitaries, who gave speeches concerning Bordeaux's illustrious Jewish Community, plus the accounts of two sisters and a gentleman who had been captured as children in Bordeaux, sent to extermination camps and, improbably, survived. Their words carried the potency of earth tides, and lifted my furtive imagination to intertwine their recollections with the moment of my grandfather's arrest.

* * *

Had it been a German or a French guard who had roused him that May of 1944? "Get up, old man! Take the suitcase you packed. It's time to move," I imagined him barking.

Perhaps my grandfather recognized the voice of his in-house jailer, but he might have wondered where he was. Had he been transferred to the Jewish nursing home along with his ailing wife, Juliette? After all, he wasn't well either after four years of sparse diet and house arrest. Or, was he, in fact, still home? He would have wanted to be home in the sole room allowed him, where he could live alongside his publications on economic history—one per year for twenty years—and next to his precious books reaching up to the tall ceilings. With those in view, it seemed he could bear anything.

Did he regret he had refused his friend, Jacques Ellul's, single realistic offer to escape? His excuse: who would look after his library? His books were the reason he avoided the round-up in January of 1944; they were too heavy to pack and cart to the Synagogue. Instead, he had folded light non-essentials into a small suitcase, set it by his bed and, inconceivably, stayed put.

In time he would have heard, but not believed (any more than he could believe that placing elderly Jews in a nursing home simply made it easier for their captors to round them up en masse), that those who were not slaughtered in the Synagogue and stripped of their possessions in January were taken away to be murdered elsewhere. In his isolated state, might gossip have filtered to him that the Vichy government was transporting Jews of all ages to undefined concentration camps in Gurs or Merignac, and then . . . elsewhere?

I wondered how assured he felt the enemy would not take him? He might have believed he had no enemies at all. After thirty-five years of teaching Law, Political Science and Economics at the University, where he had plenty of admirers among the students and professors, who would denounce him? Up until 1940 when the Statute of Jews decreed Joseph could no longer teach, or research, or write another of his many treatises, he and Professor Poplawski were colleagues together. Poplawski was influential. He would speak up for Joseph. And how about the fifteen years Joseph was adjunct mayor of the City? Adrian Marquet, the mayor whom he revered, was his friend. Joseph had been loyal, had supported Marquet through every cultural, social, economic and architectural initiative they undertook together for the City. Bordeaux thrived. Surely Marquet would defend his admirable adjunct mayor. But both Marquet and Poplawski became collaborators and did nothing to save Joseph. When did they become such cowards? Could Joseph have conjured each would become Judas?

I imagined he did not linger on what had imprisoned him for four years, but thought, instead, of the guard shoving him into a conveyance. Did Joseph wonder why no one was there to help him? Where might his son, Pierre, be? What had happened to the other son he once had? What became of him and of his sisters? They went away so early, didn't keep in touch. But nor did he. Even his students didn't like him then. But he changed. Too late. So many losses.

Did he despair over his tribe, reviled and dislocated so many times in history? Over the baseless accusations of its members being pariahs? Was Joseph's dark transport long enough to allow him to review that when his ancestors came from Portugal in the 1500s, Bordeaux was safe? How their numbers had swelled with the arrival of the Marranos? That as peddlers, or ship-builders and merchants, the Jews had educated themselves, formed charitable organizations, taken care of the poor and needy, paid a rabbi to teach the Torah?

I doubt the guard would have entered into these imagined thoughts, or that he would have shown anything but contempt for Joseph's pride over those Jews who ran for office and thought along humanitarian lines. Did Joseph want to educate his jailer to Rodrigues-Pereira, who devised an early sign language; to Abraham Furtado, who organized the Consistory of Bordeaux and became Deputy Mayor, himself; to the seven Sephardics Bordeaux sent to the States General in 1789 to ensure the Jews were granted equal rights as citizens? The powers-that-be had not killed them during the Reign of Terror, and Napoleon had supported the Jews! Whence this present hatred and vilification?

I imagined Joseph's guard shocking him from his reverie with a kick. "Get out, old man!" And then he was in Merignac with his wife, Juliette, his brother, Nathaniel, and his wife, Emma. They stayed there, increasingly degraded by scant hygiene, water or food, until the Vichy policed them into a rude railroad car, headed north to Drancy, for a few more days of dehumanization. On May 22nd 1944, three months before the liberation of Paris, these four Benzacars left Drancy crammed into Convoy Number 74, the last of the war, a cattle car that cursory hosings had not rid of the reek of vermin, soiled bodies, disease and death.

He had three days in which to block out his wife's cries for help, as well as his own. Would he have been sure he could distinguish his brother's quaver or those of Emma's? The only sustenance that diverted their crazed hunger was the thickness of their own stench. His feet and legs must have been swollen, exquisitely painful from constant standing. I wondered if his thoughts came at all, or slowly . . . staggered . . . when breath allowed . . .

when the present horror did not suffocate . . . which must have been most of the time. He was eighty-two.

When the train randomly applied its brakes, I imagined it jolted the numbed nerve endings into reawakened pain. By an attenuating thread, I wondered if he were able to hang onto his lifelong rational acts, or to any positive thoughts he could muster, because what surrounded him were surreal scenes from Hieronymus Bosch. These could not be.

Three days later, the doors opened onto a platform from which they read backwards the lettering their train had passed under: "ierF thcaM tiebrA."

* * *

I did give my speech, so rattled by the actual accounts, and by my impromptu imaginings, that the podium shook as I hung onto it.

I thanked those who faced down the lies and crimes of the collaborators in exchange for the freedoms of truth. I thanked the committee for restoring honor and recognition to my grandfather, who had contributed so significantly and so long to his city of birth. As proof, I read his own words from the letter of October, 1940, the letter that led me to his discovery, the letter that survived to prove the Nazis and the Vichy had failed, the letter that offered his own encomium. I closed with a challenge Nicole insisted I add, which was to guard against a recrudescence of France's anti-Semitism. *La vigilance s'obstine.*

While researching my grandfather's life, I found a single photograph of him. It was from a newspaper, the quality grainy and discolored with age. The photograph shows him seated and leaning slightly forward from his right shoulder. Both beautifully-shaped hands—remarkably like my father's—rest on his knees. His rather clumpy-looking dark shoes open from his heels in a V shape on the light carpet. His forehead stretches into a bald pate with hair on the sides of his rectangular head. His beard is long and his hair is dark. He is dressed in his professor's robes and he is smiling comfortably at the camera. The photo is undated, but certainly before the war. The newspaper is from Bordeaux.

I wondered if a copy of it had ever fallen into my father's hands at the time it was taken. It is the kind of photo one might find in a family trunk but, certainly, it was not among the artifacts Arlette unpacked from the one our father brought with him when he left Brazil in 1950.

It had taken long to discover grandfather Joseph, but I was so glad I had. I understood his passion for books. I wondered over his refusal to leave his library even as he risked losing his life while guarding it. Was he trusting others would be as loyal as he was towards his students, his university colleagues, his mayor? Was it courage or naïveté? I valued what he had contributed as adjunct mayor in the promotion of arts, culture and architecture in the city of his birth and ancestry. I found him both estimable and *sympa*, and grieved over the never-explained rift and ultimate loss between him and his son, our father. We all had suffered losses, but I had gained revelations and a chance to bear witness.

And if I never understood or even thought to ask about my family's silence and secrets in Brazil during the war, Nicole revealed the good sense of our parent's caution when subterfuge and dislocations were the norm, but nothing was *normale*.

* * *

In retrospect, I can't imagine I would have been able to define *normale* in my life. We had had no war on Brazilian soil, and because of my family's protection, I lived there in political ignorance.

We ex-pats were as complex and fluid as the indigenous populations that boasted Indian, African, and European ancestry, and our own multi-national family became one with them. More than anything, I feel this Brazilian culture of acceptance and inclusion was what imprinted Rio as our familial home, and Guanabara as our physical and metaphoric haven.

Leaving them physically was shearing, so I do not wish to *matar saudades, kill my longings* for the life I was lucky enough to have there in my formative years. If my conscious memory is complicated and surely inaccurate, my sensual memory is strong, reliable and full of pleasures. In unanticipated waves, it brings me back to my family in an ocean of kind people, omnipresent music, a Babel of languages, organic scents and the mutable rhythms that continue to support me. I am full of gratitude.

Genealogical Charts

Bottin Genealogy

MATERNAL SIDE

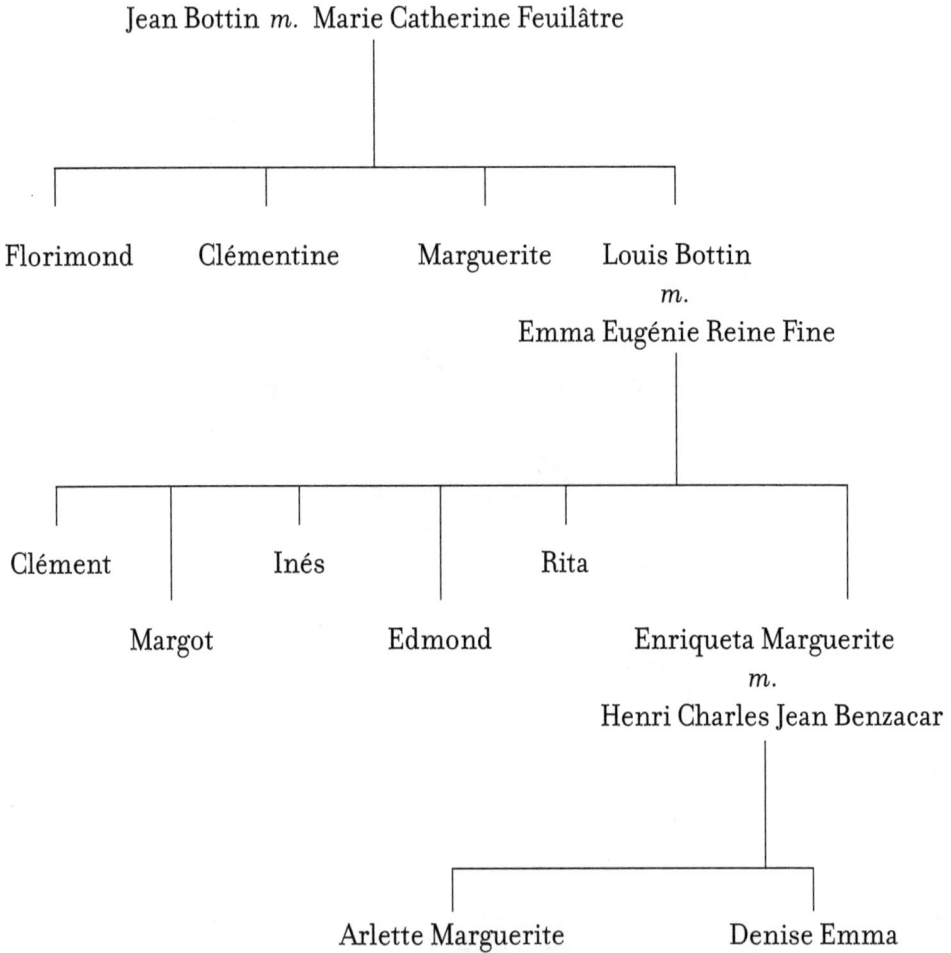

Jean Bottin *m.* Marie Catherine Feuilâtre

Florimond   Clémentine   Marguerite   Louis Bottin
m.
Emma Eugénie Reine Fine

Clément   Inés   Rita

Margot   Edmond   Enriqueta Marguerite
m.
Henri Charles Jean Benzacar

Arlette Marguerite   Denise Emma

Benzacar Genealogy

UP TO THE AUTHOR'S AND HER SISTER'S GENERATION

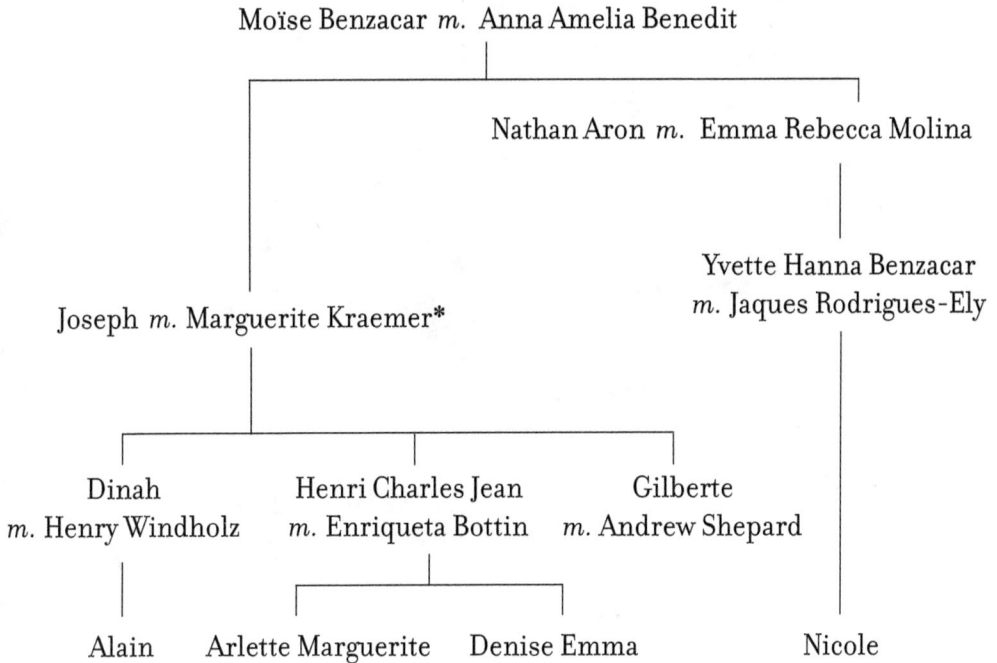

Moïse Benzacar *m.* Anna Amelia Benedit

Nathan Aron *m.* Emma Rebecca Molina

Yvette Hanna Benzacar
m. Jaques Rodrigues-Ely

Joseph *m.* Marguerite Kraemer*

Dinah
m. Henry Windholz

Henri Charles Jean
m. Enriqueta Bottin

Gilberte
m. Andrew Shepard

Alain   Arlette Marguerite   Denise Emma   Nicole

*Joseph and Marguerite divorce

Joseph Benzacar *m.* Juliette

Pierre Benzacar

Marguerite *m.* Georges Hartenstein

Jacqueline Hartenstein *m.* Michel Ferry

Alain Ferry

Acknowledgements

Unbridled thanks for seeing this idea come to fruition go to:

Ann Darby, Sandra Tyler, Nancy Woodruff, fine writers all, and first readers of my manuscript. Their patience, consideration, humor, critical advice and kindness got me to a second reading. Ann got me through to the last,

Camilla Trinchieri, who understood the voice of a transplant,

Augusta Gross, whose insights suggested following my mother's voice,

Leslie T. Sharpe, Barbara Salvatore, Virginia F. Schwartz, co-memoirists, poets, artists, naturalists and splendid editors who are definitely among my angels on earth,

Mildred Berendsen, whose steady enthusiasm, support, belief in possibilities, love and wisdom affected our entire family into three generations,

Sally Wiseley and her parents, for their enhancement of our lives in Rio and North America, and for teaching me English,

Wendy Wilson Chittenden, valued reader and friend in Rio, Montreal and New York,

Peter and Thelma Huber, Cariocas da gema e do coração,

Stefan Kanfer, author and editor extraordinaire, whose encouragement, humor, and years of fine writing helped me stick to what mattered,

Christine Kendall, **Catherine A. Lillie**, **Paul Pitcoff**, **Sidney S. Stark**, who formed a collaborative critique group of singular cohesion and invariable help,

Katie Holeman, talented book designer and fine friend,

my sister, **Arlette**, who brought me through the most difficult years without stint,

my wonderful parents, **Queta**, **Benny** and **Lou**,

Laverne and **Don Murray**, guardians who continued the Brazilian idyll in America when Arlette and I needed it most,

Nicole Rodrigues-Ely, remarkable long-lost cousin, genealogist and scribe of Benzacar lore,

Marc Malherbe, for his research and publication of *Figures d'Aquitaine: de la célébrité à l'oublie*, which shed so much light on Joseph Benzacar, and for his finding,

Jean-Pierre Duprat, who, in turn, gave me his own collection of my grandfather's writings and theses—inestimable gifts,

my glorious children, **Andrea**, **Erika** and **Seth** for their being, their shared laughter and tears, encouragement, discretion, wisdom,

Tom, husband of fifty-eight years, for still making stabs at understanding me and giving me space en route to accomplish what I need, for support laced with laughter and love,

the **New York Public Library** and its staff, endlessly superb.

About the Author

Of Brazilian-Chilean-French origins, fluent in four languages, and a traveler to the seven continents with her husband and children, Denise B. Dailey adapts easily to international subjects. Her ability to listen to people in multiple languages, and her passion to share their stories, inform and propel most of her writing, from short stories to her travel journal, *Listening to Pakistan* (2012), and her most recent award-winning biographical novel, *Riko: Seductions of an Artist* (2018), named one of 100 best reads for 2018 by Kirkus Reviews.

Denise has a B.Sc. from McGill and an MFA from Columbia Universities. In private and public schools, she has taught music, science and English, and English as a Second Language in the School of General Studies at Columbia University.

Thirty-five years ago, Denise B. Dailey and her sister Arlette unpacked a chest their father had sealed almost thirty-five years before that—when, after the death of their mother, he closed their childhood home in Rio and resettled the silently grieving family in Montreal. The chest was filled with the artifacts of their Brazilian childhood—much like the memoir Dailey has conjured, a trove of beautifully rendered memories from a magical childhood. A happy childhood, and, long before the term was coined, a multicultural childhood, for her dashing father was French and her alluring and talented mother, Chilean-French, their friends Brazilian, German, American, indigenous.

Yet childhood homes have musty cellars and secret passageways, and Dailey reveals the profound secrets stumbled upon as she wrote this story, secrets good people might keep to protect the children, secrets they might keep with the determination to live life well now.

In her previous two books—*Listening to Pakistan*, a travel memoir, and her award-wining *Riko: Seductions of an Artist*, a biography of the Czech painter Jan Emmerich Mikeska—Dailey masterfully told complex stories with wisdom, compassion, and insight. But this memoir is surely her chef d'oeuvre. It is written in stunningly graceful prose, by turns fresh as a child's voice, savvy as a young mother's, keen as a naturalist's, judicious as a rabbi's. You will fall in love with this family, and their story will break your heart.

—Ann Darby, author of *The Orphan Game*

A journey through the lush Brazilian landscape of memory and across continents to untangle family secrets amidst the abrupt loss of mother, motherland and mother tongue. This memoir takes a celebratory twist toward redemption and belonging.

— Virginia Frances Schwartz
author of *Among The Fallen* (Holiday House Fall '19)

Author of *Listening to Pakistan* and the critically-acclaimed *Riko: Seductions of an Artist*, Denise B. Dailey now gives us her memoir about growing up in Brazil during World War II and its profound effects on her life. Through her mother's letters, newspaper entries and her own sensual observations as a child, Dailey brings the reader to Rio in the 1940s, and teaches of Brazil's singular participation on the Allied side of the war. In highly evocative language (including translated passages in Portuguese, French and Spanish), Dailey treats the readers to the discovery of international secrets and family disclosures, losses and recoveries as if these revelations were the readers' own.

— Leslie T. Sharpe
author of *The Quarry Fox*, Gold Medal IPPY Award Winner

Momentum Ink Press

Momentum Ink Press is a private micro-press cooperative advancing the work of writers unavailable through traditional commercial publishers. Each book is carefully reviewed by a collection of authors and designers, ensuring an authentic artistic version of the writer's work. By selecting and reading a Momentum Ink Press book, you are joining and supporting a community of readers and writers dedicated to giving voice to talented authors purposely avoiding the commercialization of art.

www.ingramcontent.com/pod-product-compliance
Lightning Source LLC
Chambersburg PA
CBHW060235050426
42448CB00009B/1443